PROPOSAL
Writing

Second Edition

Soraya M. Coley
Cynthia A. Scheinberg

Sage Publications, Inc.
International Educational and Professional Publisher
Thousand Oaks ■ London ■ New Delhi

For information:

Sage Publications, Inc.
2455 Teller Road
Thousand Oaks, California 91320
E-mail: order@sagepub.com

Sage Publications Ltd.
6 Bonhill Street
London EC2A 4PU
United Kingdom

Sage Publications India Pvt. Ltd.
M-32 Market
Greater Kailash I
New Delhi 110 048 India

Printed in the United States of America

Library of Congress Cataloging-in-Publication Data

Coley, Soraya M. (Soraya Moore)
    Proposal writing / by Soraya M. Coley, Cynthia A. Scheinberg.— 2nd ed.
        p. cm.
    Includes bibliographical references.
    ISBN 0-7619-1959-7 (cloth: alk. paper)
    ISBN 0-7619-1960-0 (pbk.: alk. paper)
    1. Proposal writing in human services.
    2. Social service. I. Scheinberg, Cynthia A. II. Title.
    HV41 .C548 2000
    658.15′224—dc21   99-050755

This book is printed on acid-free paper.

00   01   02   03   04   05   06   7   6   5   4   3   2

Acquisition Editor:	Rolf Janke
Editorial Assistant:	Heidi Van Middlesworth
Production Editor:	Sanford Robinson
Editorial Assistant:	Victoria Cheng
Cover Designer:	Candice Harman

To Ron Coley, my husband, who supported me in all stages of this book and who had faith when I faltered, praise and inspiration when I doubted, and love and friendship always.—S.C.

To my parents, Lucille and Norman Trinkle, and my daughters, Rebecca and Rachel, for their love and support.—C.S.

CONTENTS

FOREWORD

Coley and Scheinberg have taken their outstanding guide to proposal writing, a volume popular with both students and practitioners, and made it even better. As in their first edition, they walk you through the process of proposal development and design. An expanded section on funding environments explores the implications of changing patterns of government funding and the explosive growth of mega-foundations and new voluntary sector funding sources. New opportunities abound during the first decade of the 21st century, but capitalizing on them requires knowing how to present your case to specific funders. A proposal that persuades one may turn off another.

Proposal writing is not necessarily an easy art to learn. It takes a knack, some experience, and lots of know-how. This book demystifies both the technical aspects of the process—what goes where and in what form or forms—and the marketing aspects—how to present your case in the most attractive way. A popular feature of the first edition is expanded and updated here. It includes sample proposal components and reviewer critiques.

Drawing on their own experience and those of colleagues and students, the authors show you how to present your vision, program, budget, and timetable in a direct and logical fashion. Just as valuably, they guide you in how to tailor what you have to say to a particular funder's interests.

Proposal writing and what goes on before, during, and after submission are all part of a professional process of *communication*. Communication implies bringing together; it requires sharing what we have or could have in *common*. Communication, in its fullest sense, is a reciprocal process. A well-written proposal is based on an understanding of this reciprocity. It presumes that the party or parties being communicated with have a set of interests and concerns. The proposal speaks to those interests. It further presumes a response. If the proposal is properly phrased and targeted, the response is likely to be positive, often expressed in the form of a grant or contract award.

The award itself is a form of communication, one that demands a response in terms of action and reporting, often in terms of shared planning and decision making. That may seem like a heavy load to impose on a single document. On the contrary, it is a much more modest load than inexperienced proposal writers (and old-timers like me) are sometimes likely to impose on a proposal. The point is that no proposal should be expected to say everything that could be said. It only needs to say as much as is necessary at a particular point in the exchange or communication process between funders and petitioners.

With these thoughts in mind, I invite you to share an adventure with the authors and your colleagues. Proposal writing, like any form of communication, can open up new avenues of exploration that will lead to new and important discoveries—about ourselves, our programs, and those with whom we work on the behalf of people in need.

Armand Lauffer
University of Michigan

PREFACE TO THE SECOND EDITION

Many things have changed in the human service environment since the publication of the first edition. In this second edition, we have broadened the scope of the book while making every effort to maintain those aspects of the first edition that worked. We have added a chapter on program development to help a new grantwriter understand the theoretical concepts and research aspects of writing a proposal. This edition is also updated to reflect changes in service delivery, such as collaborations, and in the use of technology in proposal writing (it is interesting for us to note that we referenced typewriters in the first edition).

In preparation for this new edition, we interviewed faculty who used the book to teach proposal writing and agency executives and grantwriters. We have incorporated many of their suggestions into this edition.

Like the first edition, this book is written primarily for students or beginning to moderately experienced grantwriters working in nonprofit corporations, school districts, or city or county agencies. In our work with both public and private health and human service agencies, we repeatedly heard the need for a guide on conceptualizing *and* writing grants. We hope our response to that need is useful and supports the efforts of those who are seeking the resources to improve the human condition!

We are grateful to the following individuals for their contributions of advice, expertise, and collegial support for this second edition: Michelle Berelowitz, Nancee Buck, Sid Gardner, Carol Geisbauer, Jo Gottfried, and Dan McQuaid. The support of Dr. Milton A. Gordon, President of California State University Fullerton (CSUF), Nora Velarde, Dean's Secretary, and the faculty and staff of the College of Human Development and Community Service at California State University Fullerton is also acknowledged.

Similarly, we continue to derive inspiration from the faculty and students of proposal writing classes at CSUF, whose requests for clarification of certain concepts helped us to see where the text needed revision. We are further inspired by those students who have gone on to write proposals and have their programs funded—this, of course, provides us with a deep sense of satisfaction.

The Grantwriter's Plea

Grant me the courage to write and submit a grant,
the serenity to deal with the denial of the grant,
the wisdom to know whether to revise and resubmit the grant. . .
Please Grant Me a Grant!!!

S. Coley and C. Scheinberg

1

AN ORIENTATION TO PROPOSAL WRITING

Chapter Highlights

♦ Definitions
♦ How to Find Grant Applications
♦ The Ingredients of a Proposal
♦ The Process of Submitting a Proposal
♦ The Difference Between Grants and Contracts
♦ Technology and Proposal Writing
♦ Organizing the Writing
♦ Writing Style and Format

DEFINITIONS

A *proposal* is a written document prepared in application for funding. The individual who prepares the proposal is called a *proposal writer* or *grantwriter*. The state, federal, or corporate resource to whom the proposal is submitted is called a *funder*. The proposals we address in this book are those prepared by nonprofit organizations to state or federal offices, foundations, and corporations to provide community-based services.

When an agency receives funding, it is said that the agency "got a grant," although technically speaking, it most likely "got a contract." In this book, we will use the everyday convention—we'll help you "write a grant!"

HOW TO FIND GRANT APPLICATIONS

Grants are available primarily through three types of funding sources: governmental agencies, foundations, and corporations. The following section will help you to understand the different types of applications and where they are located.

GOVERNMENTAL APPLICATIONS

When a governmental agency has available funds, it issues a *Funding Announcement*, which provides the information needed to obtain a *Request for Applications (RFA)* or *Request for Proposals (RFP)*. (We recently saw a funder put out an RFS, or Request for Services.) This RFA/RFP is the application packet containing full instructions and all of the required forms needed to submit the proposal. Funding announcements for the federal government can be found in publications such as the *Federal Register* or at each of the home page sites for governmental agencies. There are many governmental offices issuing funding announcements, such as the Department of Health and Human Services and the Centers for Disease Control. (See Appendix B for Funding Resource Information.)

FOUNDATION APPLICATIONS

Most not-for-profit foundations have written guidelines for the submission of proposals that can be obtained through a phone call or letter requesting the guidelines or at the foundation's home page. There are publications that compile listings of foundation programs such as the *Guide to Foundations*. This useful resource is also available on CD-ROM and is searchable by topic and may be owned by libraries in your area. Foundations generally receive proposals two to four times per year, and some foundations accept proposals by invitation only. Some foundations focus their work on a local level, others on a regional level (e.g., Southern California), and still others nationally.

CORPORATE AND CORPORATE
FOUNDATION APPLICATIONS

There are a broad range of corporate giving programs, from the small business donation determined by the owner to formally structured corporate foundations with boards of directors and program officers. Almost every large corporation has some form of community giving program. In many cases, there is a link to the corporate giving program through the company home page. One can also get information about corporate giving programs through contact with company employees, brochures in the store, and public announcements in newspapers or magazines. Corporations have written guidelines for their application process and generally receive proposals quarterly.

THE INGREDIENTS OF A PROPOSAL

Proposals are a communication tool enabling applicants to express the needs of their local community, the value of the proposed services, and the expertise and capability of the applicant agency to the funder. The following sections are included as standard format in most grant proposals:

1. *Cover Letter, Title Page, and/or Abstract*: Introduces the project and agency to the funder.
2. *Needs Statement (also called the Problem Statement* or *Case Study)*: Describes the community to be served and the problem or need being addressed by the proposal.
3. *Project Description*: Includes goals and objectives and provides details about the implementation plan. This section often includes a *Scope of Work* grid of the project delivery plan.
4. *Evaluation Plan*: Explains the measurement procedures that will be used to determine if goals and objectives have been met.
5. *Budget Request*: Itemizes the expenditures of the project and includes a rationale or budget justification for the expenses.
6. *Applicant Capability*: Demonstrates the applicant's past performance and ability to accomplish the proposed project.
7. *Future Funding Plans*: Indicates the plan to continue the project beyond the requested funding period.
8. *Letters of Support*: Letters reflecting community support for the proposed project from program recipients, community leaders, agencies, schools, and/or religious organizations.
9. *Memoranda of Understanding*: A written agreement from each of the partners or coapplicant agencies included in this grant application.
10. *Appendix Materials*: These may include an audited financial statement, insurance documentation, or any other documentation required by the funder.

THE PROCESS OF SUBMITTING
A PROPOSAL

There are several steps involved in submitting a proposal. This process is illustrated in Figure 1.1.

Most governmental funders and many foundations require potential applicants to submit a *letter of intent* to apply for funding and bar applicants who have not announced their interest in the process from proceeding. Some use the letter of intent to screen potential applicants and ensure the submission of appropriate proposals. You will find this process explained in the funding announcement or in a cover letter supplied by the funder.

In addition to the submission of a letter of intent, the federal government often requires that applicants notify the state government about the funding request they are making. In this case, instructions are also in the application packet and describe who to make contact with and when. (This is sometimes called a *single point of contact* request or SPOC.) It may suffice to send a copy of the proposal to the SPOC when the application is submitted to the federal office. We also recommend that you send a copy to your local legislators so they can advocate on your behalf.

Once you have filed the letter of intent, you will be notified as to the dates and locations of any *bidders' conferences* designed to enhance your understanding of the goals of the funder and of specific details in proposal preparation. The bidders' conference gives the funder the opportunity to clarify the intent of the proposal and to answer questions about the proposal in as fair a manner as possible. Prospective applicants receive a written transcript of the proceedings of all of the conferences held by the funder. The conference also provides an opportunity to learn which other agencies are interested in submitting an application, leading to possible cooperative proposals and assessment of the competition. It is customary for the funder to provide a roster of attendees at the bidders' conference to others in attendance.

The proposal must be received by the potential funder by the deadline date. Submission deadlines will be included in the announcement and will determine the time frame for proposal preparation. Many governmental funders allow approximately 4 to 6 weeks between the funding announcement and the proposal due date. Funders are very serious about submission due dates, and we are aware of many sad stories of agency personnel running the grant into the office at 1 minute after the deadline and being turned away.

Once the proposal is submitted and it has undergone a preliminary review, some foundation funders will make site visits to meet the board

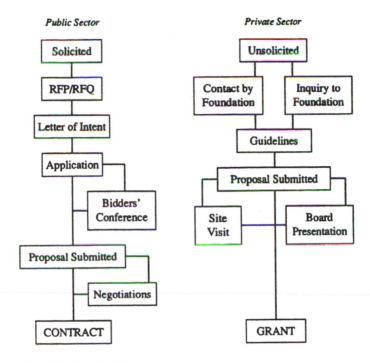

Figure 1.1. The Funding Process

and staff members and ensure that the agency is doing what it has indicated in the proposal. In some cases, the agency may be invited to make a presentation to the foundation's board of directors.

A notification of award is usually mailed by the funder to the applicant. In cases where the application is rejected and the proposal not funded, it is often possible to receive the scoring and reviewers' comments. This is very helpful and strongly encouraged. On occasion, an agency may contest the outcome of the application process. Most governmental funders have a grievance process to follow if the applicant believes there is an error or oversight or seeks to contest the determination. Details regarding this process will be found in the RFA packet.

In the best case, an award letter will arrive, indicating that the application was successful and announcing the award amount. Often, this amount is less than applied for, and applicants will enter into negotiations with the funder. During these negotiations, the project description section and the budget section of the proposal will be modified to reflect the level of effort required under the funded amount.

THE DIFFERENCE BETWEEN
GRANTS AND CONTRACTS

In the "Definitions" section of this chapter, we provided a simplified definition of a grant. When you deal with a county, state, or federal funder, your successful proposal will most likely result in a contract. Technically speaking, a *grant* is assistance given to an organization (or individual) to accomplish its (his/her) stated purposes and objectives. On the other hand, a *contract* represents a procurement or purchase arrangement in which the contracting agency "buys" services from the organization (or individual) to fulfill the contracting agency's obligations or responsibilities. In this case, the agency becomes an agent of the funder (Kettner & Martin, 1987; Lauffer, 1997). The following examples highlight the distinction. Examples of a contract are:

- The federal government contracts with a consortium of agencies to provide health care screening and information/education to parents of children under 6 years of age.
- The state government secures employment training for recipients of public aid through a contract with a private, nonprofit agency.
- The county government contracts with a nonprofit agency to provide counseling and shelter for abused and neglected children.

Examples of a grant are:

- A nonprofit, youth-serving agency receives a grant from a corporation to increase program recipients' knowledge about the dangers of drug and alcohol abuse.
- A family service agency receives funding through a foundation to expand its parent education program.
- A collaborative receives a grant for a child abuse prevention program.

Under a contractual arrangement, the governmental bodies are legally mandated to provide services for their program recipients (e.g., recipients of public aid, or abused and neglected children). They must decide whether to provide the services directly through a public institution or indirectly through a nonprofit or for-profit vendor. In the examples above, they have contracted with nonprofit agencies to provide care and/or services. In these instances, those served are considered program recipients of the government, and the contracted agency is required to abide by all governmental mandates. Contracts are a legally binding promise to provide specified services.

In the grant aid examples, the nonprofit agencies received monies to provide services to their program recipients within their own policies and guidelines. Grant monies can be thought of as "awards in good faith," usually requiring less documentation of programmatic effort over the award term and allowing more flexibility in daily operations than contracts.

TECHNOLOGY AND PROPOSAL WRITING

Computers, the Internet, e-mail, and faxes have revolutionized the way that information is gathered for the preparation and writing of a proposal. Computer literacy, an e-mail account, a fax machine, and access to the World Wide Web are requirements for today's grantwriter.

Many funding announcements can be found at government or corporate home pages. You can find these pages by using a search engine such as Yahoo!, Excite, or Alta Vista and looking for the company or government office you want. There is an exciting new Web site called "Grants, Etc" that provides a comprehensive and simple-to-use introduction to funding sources, in-kind resources, electronic journals, and how-to guides. You can find this site at *http://www.ssw.umich.edu/grantsetc*. When you are just beginning or looking for new funding sources, network with other professionals in the field who can help connect you to specific funding sources. (See Appendix B for more Internet addresses.) Searches on the Internet can yield interesting results, from research articles and other statistical data to new funding sources.

Once you have located a funding source, the next step is to download the RFA package from the host site. In most cases, this will require that you have a "reader" for the text to be delivered to you. (One of the standard readers on the market today is Adobe Acrobat, and it can be ordered from Adobe or downloaded from the Adobe home page at *http://www.adobe.com*.) Downloading large applications can take a couple of hours. Once you have received the files, you can print the application.

In addition to "surfing" the Web to find new funding opportunities, you may subscribe to "listservs," which are like big mailing lists. You can, for example, be placed on a listserv for the Department of Health's RFAs and receive announcements to your e-mail address as soon as they are released.

An innovation in proposal submission can be seen at corporate Web sites, where you may find and submit a grant application entirely over the Web! This format is so simple that it makes grantwriting fun.

A pesky and potentially serious problem associated with being on the Internet is the possibility of contracting a virus. We recommend that you purchase a current antivirus software program with on-line update capability and use it regularly. You should also stay updated in relation to the viruses sent via e-mail so you don't inadvertently open a message and activate a virus. Your Internet host site will post warnings about these viruses as they come onto the scene.

ORGANIZING THE WRITING

The following section is for the beginning proposal writer and addresses some of the issues associated with general organization and work habits. Individuals who have written proposals before will be very aware of the usual obstacles and barriers that greet the writer along the way. As most proposals are written under the pressure of deadlines (which are almost always too short), organization becomes critical.

In today's climate, proposals are most often written by more than one person. If the proposal is being written by a collaborative or partnership, there may be one administrator and a grantwriter from the lead agency and one or two others from participating agencies. If a sole agency is writing the proposal, a grantwriter, an executive director, a program director, and program staff may be involved in the writing. Whatever the configuration, there is usually one main writer. This "point person" pulls it all together into one style, ensures that all of the extra materials are gathered up for inclusion into the grant, and makes certain that the grant application is in the format required by the funder. It will be the job of the main writer to read the RFA carefully and in minute detail.

As many things begin to happen simultaneously in the writing process, we can't overemphasize the need for a place to work that allows for the undisturbed storage of materials. Think of what it is like to write a term paper—your research is spread out on the table, your drafts are piled up next to it, and your books are spread open on the floor. When writing the proposal, you may have one pile for the data related to the problem, another for work plans from your agency and other agencies if you are collaborating, another for budgets from each of those agencies, and still another for support letters or other documentation from each participating agency. Many people we know use boxes to contain the components of a particular project; others use notebooks.

The best grantwriter will use an editor. In most cases, this will be someone who has worked with the grantwriter in preparing the proposal so that he or she is familiar with the project. The editor will help to ensure that the main ideas in the proposal are clearly stated and that the proposal is internally consistent. All of the numerical totals in budgets should be double-checked by the editor as well. Finally, the editor will double-check to ensure that all attachments are included and that the proposal is assembled accurately.

We have mentioned timelines that are imposed by the funder, but the grantwriter must also be aware of other processes through which the grant application must pass before being ready for submission. Will the application need to be approved by the board of directors of the agency? By the board of directors of partner or collaborating agencies? Organizing a proposal requires an awareness of all of the different time lines to which the proposal may be subject.

It is worth the time and energy it takes to ensure adequate supplies for the writing process in advance. Purchase extra printer, fax and copier paper, copier toner, printer ink, stamps, large envelopes, white-out, file folders, index cards, pens, and large butterfly clips. Have overnight express mailers preaddressed and stamped in preparation for a last-minute rush. Know where you can go to use a copier if yours breaks at the last minute, and *always back up your work onto a disk.* (Remember to scan the disk for viruses every time it changes hands from one writer to another before reinstalling the proposal on your computer.)

Fifty percent of the proposals funded are resubmissions that were denied the first time. This statement is not made to discourage you but rather to ground you a bit in the reality of the process. Because this is a highly competitive business, grantwriters learn not to take rejection personally. In fact, too much personal investment in the proposal can work to your disadvantage, as you may lose the objectivity needed to negotiate the proposal, make modifications, or even learn from mistakes.

WRITING STYLE AND FORMAT

Although not stated in the RFA, proposals that are written to governmental funding sources and some large foundations require a formal writing style. However, unlike a research paper in which you use footnotes or endnotes to cite references, the references are usually incorporated into the body of the text. For example, one might write, "In 1999, the birth rate for adolescents ages 15 to 17 in Orange County, California, was 38.5 per thousand (Orange County Health Care Agency)" or "According to a recent study conducted by the Children's Defense Fund (Annual Report, 1999), latchkey children are at greater risk for stress-related disorders." We hypothesize that this style of referencing developed as a practical response to space restrictions: With a limited number of pages in which to present a case, grantwriters are likely to resist devoting one to references. In proposals in which there is adequate space, we recommend that you use a standard reference style such as APA and attach references.

Formal writing requires that you write to the most intelligent of audiences and eliminate informal references or comments such as "I think" or "it seems to me that. . . ." What is stated as fact in the text needs to be referenced as such, and only factual statements should be included in the writing. For the most part, the reviewer of the proposal will be a professional in the field who is well educated and experienced on the issue. You will be expected to use professional terminology and use it appropriately.

A proposal prepared for many foundations or corporations will often be much less complex than one prepared for the federal or state government. Some funders may require the proposal to be only three to six pages in length. Typically, the proposal is written in a less technical and more journalistic style, as the reader is more likely to be an educated "generalist" and not a specialist in the field. It is recommended that in these proposals, the writer avoid the use of professional jargon, as it interferes with the reader's overall understanding of the proposal.

In all cases, the final proposal should be clean and free of spelling or grammatical errors. It should be visually pleasing, with consistent section headers and typeface of a size and font that are easy to read (think of the reader who has six of these to evaluate!). Charts, tables, graphs, and other illustrations can enhance the impact of the proposal and are now widely used. Avoid using shading or color graphs that do not copy well, as a poor copy will detract from your proposal. (You may be able to insert shaded or color copies into each copy of the proposal in your packet if you think that the funder will not need to make additional copies to distribute to the readers.)

2

UNDERSTANDING THE AGENCY AND FUNDING ENVIRONMENT

Chapter Highlights

- ◆ Understanding the Agency
- ◆ Understanding the Funding Environment
- ◆ Other Funding Considerations
- ◆ Proposal Scoring
- ◆ Focus on Collaboration
- ◆ Writing a Proposal for a Collaborative

UNDERSTANDING THE AGENCY

In most cases, when you receive an RFP, the funder has stated goals and objectives, or a rationale for funding that articulates the type of outcomes wanted as a result of the funding. The agency, on the other hand, is looking to find funding that fits within its mission and purpose. The better the match between the funder's rationale for funding and the agency's mission and programs, the more likely the project will be funded.

It is helpful to think of the agency, the community, and the funder as being mirrors. As you hold the proposal up to each of these sectors, different aspects of the mandates of each will be reflected back to you, influencing and shaping the proposal as it unfolds.

Every agency's purpose is expressed in a mission or purpose state-ment and is reflected back into the community through the types of pro-grams it provides. Usually, the mission statement is fairly broad or global, identifying the major issue the agency focuses on and a basic philosophy of how it will address it. The mission statement is dynamic: It changes over time to adapt to emerging needs in the community. Purpose statements are elaborations on the mission statement and offer more specific information about the approach or programs that the agency will use to meet its mission. The mission and purpose statements are developed by the board of directors of the agency (in voluntary agencies) or by other governing bodies (in public agencies), who create policy statements framing the agency's scope and its general approach to the broad problem.

Most agencies have paid staff who turn the legislative body's or the board's vision and policy statements into viable programs that accomplish the agency's mission. In the case of a nonprofit agency, the executive director is responsible for developing the agency's services and implementing them in the community. The executive director is also the link between the board and the staff; therefore, it is vitally important that you work closely with this person or his or her designated alternate to develop the proposal.

Reviewing the agency's purpose, past and current programs, and future directions is a useful process. The following "survey of the organization" provides a format for examining the organization, including its current state and its strengths and weaknesses. The information you will obtain through this process will help you to develop a proposal that will move the agency forward with consistency and balance. Areas to be covered include

- History and mission statement of the agency
- Service area of the agency (geographic area)
- Population served by the agency (program recipients)
- Current programs
- Current staffing of the agency: What is the educational background and experience of key staff?
- Future plans for the agency: Where does the agency see itself 5 years from now?
- Funding sources: Is there a variety of funding coming into the agency?
- Other agencies providing similar services: the existing competition and potential for partnerships or collaboration in the current marketplace
- Contacts and connections: board member and staff relationships with potential funders

Once you have completed this survey, you will have a better understanding of the agency. Agencies are all at various levels of sophistication within their focus areas, and your proposal must fit in at a "doable" level or provide for the necessary development to reach the new level. Consider the following example. An agency has been providing educational programs to youth in schools and now wants to develop after-school programs for teens. The agency does not have the community contacts with youth-serving providers and is therefore missing a major link needed to implement the new program in a new environment. The proposal must allow for the development of this new network for the program to be successful.

UNDERSTANDING THE FUNDING ENVIRONMENT

Most funding sources also have missions or mandates to follow. In the case of governmental entities, the mandates are developed through the legislative process, and the resultant funding is allocated to address the identified need. Corporations and foundations may exist to meet certain needs, as in the case of health foundations that were developed out of the transition from nonprofit status to for-profit status. Other corporations may target particular issue areas they want to address, such as youth, education, and domestic violence.

Most funders want something in return for their giving. In some cases, this may be increased visibility and good will in a local community; in others, perhaps giving leads to increased revenue. An example of this type of strategy can be seen in credit card use linked to charitable giving: If you use a certain card, the charity will receive a percentage of your total purchase. Corporations are likely to view proposals favorably if they meet their own internal needs or promote the corporate image in the community. When writing these proposals, be aware of the "WIFM" rule ("What's in it for me?"), and work to design a program having clear benefits to the corporation as well as the agency but, most important, to those you are serving.

OTHER FUNDING CONSIDERATIONS

In addition to a well-written proposal, foundations give consideration to other factors in their decision-making process. We surveyed 164 foundations, who ranked the following as the top factors affecting whether an agency gets funded. The agency

- Demonstrates a positive and measurable impact on those being served
- Is a collaborative or partnership
- Indicates a cost-effective operation
- Supports other organizations in the community
- Reflects cultural sensitivity and diversity
- Focuses on primary prevention of the problem
- Has a proven track record
- Establishes new, innovative programs
- Receives funding from other sources
- Has a previous relationship with the foundation
- Has a reputation that is not too radical
- Has competent and professionally trained staff

In addition, the foundations revealed that two of the most common weaknesses in proposals are (a) no clear identification and substantiation of a significant problem and (b) a lack of clarity as to how funds are to be spent for project activities.

PROPOSAL SCORING

Typically, government funding agencies use a weighting system when reviewing proposals, with various weights or points assigned to each section of the proposal. The review criteria and the weighting system to be used are sometimes listed in the agency's program announcements or application packets. Foundations and corporations identify their proposal evaluation criteria through funding announcements but are less likely to indicate the point values assigned to specific proposal sections.

In reviewing the proposal scoring criteria used by public and private funders supporting human service programs, we found that they generally weighted the proposal sections in the following order:

1. Project Approach, including goals, outcomes, and project activities
2. Needs/Problem Statement
3. Budget
4. Agency Capability
5. Evaluation Methods

Funders are looking for projects that are realistic, have measurable outcomes with a good chance for success, and are ambitious. It is always attractive if the program reaches beyond known boundaries into unknown or untried arenas in efforts that, if successful, will be a step into the future for the organization (and a nice feather in the cap of the funder).

Many times, one "well-placed" proposal has a greater possibility of being funded than one scattered indiscriminately to a variety of funders (in a practice sometimes known as "shotgunning"). Foundation and corporate development consultants are in contact with one another; they are aware of a proposal that has been circulated in this manner and look less favorably upon it.

FOCUS ON COLLABORATION

Collaboration represents new thinking about the way services are delivered. In the past, agencies provided a set of services to their identified client base, usually across large geographical areas. Although these services were vital and necessary, they often were not sufficient to fully address the problem or meet the complex needs of the client. Furthermore, to access the services of Agency X, a program recipient called a main office and transported him- or herself to the service site (sometimes many miles away). This type of service delivery structure resulted in an uneven distribution of services across large geographic areas and a fragmentation of services. Like specialization in the medical field, it left consumers seeking a way to get their needs met in one place. With this "shotgun" approach to program delivery, it was difficult to determine the total amount of resources allocated to any one problem area or given population.

In the 1990s, corporate mergers became common in both the public and private sectors as an effort to bring escalating costs under control and to add "value" to products and services. Agencies and funders began to look for new ways to deliver services more economically and efficiently, as well as with more accountability for the results of services. It became common to hear funders use the term *outcome driven* and state that "it is no longer good enough to do good in our communities. We have limited resources, and we need to know what works."

Over the past several years, the federal and state governments have released more funding to the county level. Most counties have chosen to meet the needs of the public through linkages with both public and private entities. In turn, new partnerships and collaborations have been developed on the local level to meet the needs of clients and funder alike.

In the collaborative model, *community* is redefined to better reflect an actual interactive unit of individuals, such as a religious community, a school community, or a neighborhood, rather than the broad geographical areas designated in the past, such as "the Orange County community" or the "Los Angeles community." Service "hubs" located within the smaller community are created with an overarching vision of "one-stop shopping" for program recipients. These "hubs" are often known as family resource centers. Agencies bring their services to the family resource center and forge linkages with the community surrounding the center (see Figure 2.1).

As you can imagine, collaboratives can be structured in many different ways. Figure 2.2 shows a collaborative serving a large geographic area, with services linked to school sites and community sites. In this case, the client receives services at a neighborhood facility, and the collaborative providers take their services from place to place.

Collaboration involves both advantages and challenges. The advantages of collaboration include

- Better knowledge of what services exist in a given area and what services are needed (service gaps)
- More effective in meeting the interrelated and multiple needs of program recipients
- More partnering between agencies, resulting in new and creative service delivery plans: for example, linkage of the nutrition education classes of one agency to the parenting education classes of another
- Evaluation of the collaborative as a whole, providing the opportunity to see what difference multiple services make to a single program recipient
- Increased access to program recipients
- Increased ability to track the total amount of financial resources in a given geographic area
- The development of personal relationships among providers to facilitate referrals
- Increased participation of program recipients in service delivery planning
- Increased access to local data (studies conducted by agencies or schools) and shared past proposals to help write the need statement for current proposals

The challenges of collaboration include

- Significant time spent in planning and at meetings
- The fact that some funding structures are not yet adapted to fund collaboratives with flexibility
- Potential problems between agencies regarding service planning and delivery structures
- Sharing of resources and shared responsibility for a mutual set of outcomes

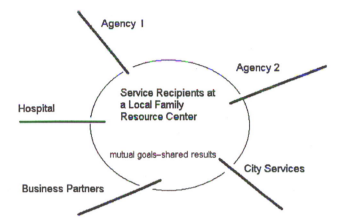

Figure 2.1. Collaborative Model Using a Single Site for Service Delivery

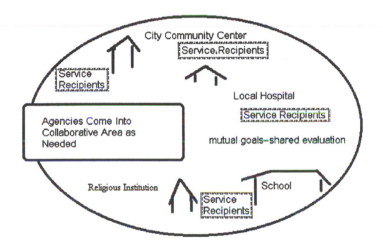

Figure 2.2. Collaborative Model Using Multiple Sites for Service Delivery

Collaboratives are living partnerships of people and bureaucracies. To be successful, the collaborative must have a shared vision, mutually developed goals, trust in the word of its leadership, a broad representation of collaborative members at the leadership level, and the ability to select and change leadership if necessary. Furthermore, the collaborative involves community members who receive services in important aspects of its functioning. According to Sid Gardner, in *Beyond Collaboration to*

Results (1999), "A successful collaborative must, almost by definition, have the capacity to tap the energies and resources of the community beyond the budgets of its members" (p. 71).

WRITING A PROPOSAL FOR
A COLLABORATIVE

When writing a proposal for a collaborative, the grantwriter should be intimately involved in all phases of development to facilitate an understanding of the many aspects of the project and capture the richness of the effort. In some cases, the grantwriter may be called upon to help develop the project and the proposal. One of the authors has led a large collaborative for the past 8 years and has developed a model for conceptualizing proposals in a large group. The following provides a brief summary of the three-part model that can be used by the grantwriter to help the collaborative members organize their thoughts and services prior to writing.

PHASE I: DETERMINING THE NEED
AND ESTABLISHING GOALS

In this phase, program recipients and service providers define the needs. At one meeting all together or through several smaller meetings, the community and service providers create goals and place needs under the appropriate goals. For example, there may be a need for immunizations and dental care in the community as well as a concern about gang violence. Two goals could be developed, one addressing the health and mental health needs of children and the other addressing community safety. The committees can make as many goals as they choose or can use the goals provided by the funder under which local services can be organized. Once the goals are completed and needs listed underneath, the committees are asked to rank the community needs from "most important to address now" to "least important to address now." (The definition and ranking of needs will help determine the asset allocation to follow.)

PHASE II: EXPLORING POSSIBLE PROGRAM
OFFERINGS AND BENEFITS

In this phase, service providers propose what they want to do to address the needs, indicate which goal they want to adderess, identify expected results and benefits, develop a budget, and provide a rationale for using this approach. In other words, are there any data or research to support the possible effectiveness of the approach in reducing or eliminating the problem?

PHASE III: DEVELOPING THE FINAL PROGRAM AND BUDGET

The program offerings are listed under the goal areas. The amount of funding requested is placed alongside each program offering. The column is totaled, and, invariably, the budget needed exceeds the funder's allocation. Using the ranking system developed by the community and service providers, the whole group makes decisions about what will stay as proposed, what might be adjusted, and what will be eliminated from the proposal.

This process allows true collaboration to occur. In many instances, agencies are able to contribute some services "in kind," meaning that they will not receive money for these services but will instead pay for the services they are tying into the proposal. (By the way, some funders require a certain percentage of the proposal to be in-kind contributions. We will address this issue further in Chapter 7 of this book.) Furthermore, in this model, all agencies are part of the decision-making process, and the lead agency of the collaborative serves as a facilitator of the process. The following chapter provides a process for more in-depth conceptualization of proposal ideas.

3

NEEDS-BASED PROGRAM DEVELOPMENT

Chapter Highlights

♦ Understanding the Community Through Data
♦ Understanding Barriers to Service
♦ Program Design and Theoretical Orientations
♦ Conceptualizing Program Ideas
♦ Sustainability and Transferability

UNDERSTANDING THE COMMUNITY THROUGH DATA

Have you ever gone without medical or dental care because you couldn't afford it? Have you seen homeless mentally ill persons pushing shopping carts up your city streets? These are examples of community needs because they affect the quality of life of the population of a geographic area. Other examples include the incidence of HIV infection, the number of babies born with birth defects, the number of persons who go to bed hungry, the incidence of high school dropouts, the incidence of domestic violence or date rape, and the quality of air or water. In short, there is a problem in the community that requires attention, and this problem is expressed as a need.

An essential first step in determining the focus of your program is to assess the needs of the community and its resources that can support your efforts in addressing the problem. To document community need (i.e., to show research, demographic data, or other scientific evidence that the problem exists), the grantwriter may become involved in conducting research as well as locating various sources of existing data. The following samples of data collection categories will provide you with a guide to the kind of data useful in both developing programmatic ideas and writing the needs statement:

- Data on the incidence of the needs/problem—whether the need has increased, has decreased, or remains the same—and clients' current physical, emotional, social, and/or economic status
- Data depicting the factors contributing to or causing the problem and data on related problems
- Data comparing the need in your target area with that in other cities, counties, your state, and other states
- Data on the short- and/or long-term consequences of no intervention (including cost analysis if available)
- Data on the activities and outcomes of other organizations responding to the same or similar need
- Data evidencing a demand for service: waiting lists, requests for service, lack of culturally appropriate services, and costs
- Data from experts in the field, including research studies on effective intervention strategies and evaluation results

The following sections help you to identify sources for the types of data previously described.

CLIENT NEEDS ASSESSMENT

A needs assessment gathers information about the client's perception of the problem and client needs. This type of assessment is usually conducted through interviews with program recipients, focus groups, or questionnaires. Many agencies, such as a local health care council or a United Way, have conducted needs assessments and may be able to share the results with you. These documents are invaluable for making a case for your project. If you conduct an assessment on your own, it is important to involve members of various ethnic groups (stakeholders) who experience the problem and who will benefit from the proposed program, as well as individuals who serve this population. You may find that there are different perspectives on the problem and its possible solutions. (To read more about conducting a client needs assessment, see Soriano, 1995.)

CITY, COUNTY, AND STATE DEMOGRAPHIC DATA

Most county governments and universities compile information about the residents in geographic areas based on census data. This demographic information includes such statistics as the number of single-parent households, the income level, the number of children, educational level, and housing density. Some university-based research centers have "geo-mapping" capabilities that allow a user to define a geographic area and extract demographic data and other indicators for that region.

Specific problems or issues are often tracked by county government and by state departments working in those issue areas. Teen pregnancy rates, for example, may be found at the county health care agency, or child abuse rates at the county department of social services. Community-based organizations will frequently have data already compiled on certain community problems. The most organized of these agencies will have the incidence of the problem at the local level (city and/or county), the state level, and the national level. It is frequently necessary to determine how your geographic area's needs compare to those of other areas.

JOURNAL ARTICLES

There is a rich storehouse of information in scientific journals. You will find research into the causes of problems as well as research on effective solutions to the problems. Journal articles will help to provide the grant-writer with the rationale for a particular program design, with program ideas, and with evaluation ideas. In addition, the bibliographies in the articles in academic journals can help a newcomer to a particular field find other important work quickly. Many journals are now accessible through the Internet.

LOCAL NEWSPAPERS

Articles in local newspapers can help the grantwriter to develop a sense of the community perception of the problem and of local resources. (The grantwriter must be cautioned not to depend solely on newspaper reports, as these articles are only as accurate as their informants.)

UNDERSTANDING BARRIERS TO SERVICE

An individual whose quality of life has been impaired by a disease process most often sees improvement once he or she obtains treatment. When, for example, a child is treated for a painful ear infection, the child feels better, the parents are happy that their child is well again and that the mother is able to return to work, and the teacher may remark that the child is doing

much better in school. These are examples of outcomes that were the result
of the medical intervention. (The ability to recognize and state program
recipient outcomes will be very important for the development of the
evaluation section of the proposal.)

However, there may have been several reasons why the child did not
see a doctor sooner to resolve the painful infection. Perhaps the parents
were without the financial resources to pay for a visit to the doctor, or
maybe they had no transportation to the clinic. Perhaps they spoke a
language other than English and feared they would not be understood.
The reasons why a client does not access services are known as *barriers*
to service.

Barriers may exist as a result of a client's orientation to services—that
is, the client may lack the knowledge, desire, or skills necessary to seek
treatment or prevent a problem. An example of this type of barrier exists in
drug treatment services when the client denies that he or she has a problem.
The client may also hold attitudes or beliefs that are not compatible with
seeking certain types of services. For example, an individual who uses traditional cultural healers may not value the services offered by Western
doctors. Often, however, barriers are created by the service providers
themselves or through the program design. These are usually assessed in
five domains:

1. *Availability*: Services may not be provided in your community, or the cost
   may be prohibitive. To what extent do professionals (e.g., nurses, social
   workers, teachers, counselors, probation officers) work together as a
   team?

2. *Accessibility*: Can the client get to the site? Does it take special physical
   needs into consideration such as handicapped access? Are the hours of
   operation convenient for the client? Is there transportation to and from the
   site? Are there eligibility criteria that may influence accessibility? To what
   extent are multiple services provided at a convenient single location?

3. *Acceptability*: Is the service pleasing to the client? Are the staff perceived as
   friendly, professional, competent, and helpful? Are the decor and design of
   the service setting inviting to and respectful of the client? Are the services in
   the client's language and sensitive to cultural issues? Are the client's physical needs taken into consideration?

4. *Appropriateness*: Is this the right service for the client? Is the service within
   the scope of the provider's ability and/or range of practice?

5. *Adequacy*: Is the service sufficient in amount to meet the community's
   needs? Are services as comprehensive as possible?

PROGRAM DESIGN AND THEORETICAL ORIENTATIONS

But what about those troubling behaviors or situations upon which a shot or medication has no impact—issues such as domestic violence, teen pregnancy, elder abuse, and homelessness, to name just a few? How does one go about proposing a solution to these problems? Theoretical frameworks, which are brought forth through research and practice, help us to understand causes and posit possible solutions to social problems. The theory about how your proposed intervention will achieve desired results is your *theory of change*. Time should be spent reflecting on the outcomes you desire as well as those created by others. In the following paragraphs, we will summarize two theoretical models or perspectives that are frequently used in program design and development to create a theory of change on which the proposal is built.

SOCIAL LEARNING THEORY

A researcher in cognitive and behavioral psychology, Albert Bandura, is a proponent of "social learning theory," which looks at the influence of the environment on the individual and offers a strategy to address the changing of social norms through cognitive and behavioral restructuring (Bandura, 1986).

An example of community programming that uses social learning theory as a foundation for program design is provided by antismoking campaigns. For years, the campaign hammered away at the community with an antitobacco message stating that smoking was bad for your health. When the campaign was able to leverage peer pressure on smokers with messages that smoking compromised the health of others, and when it created public pressure for smoke-free workplaces, restaurants, and bars, there was a shift in societal norms, and it became unacceptable to smoke.

STAGES OF CHANGE

As we know from experience, change occurs over time. Well-known researchers (Prochaska, Norcross, & DiClemente, 1994) proposed a series of six stages that people go through as they try to change troubling behavior (their research was conducted with people who were trying to quit smoking): (a) precontemplation, (b) contemplation, (c) preparation, (d) action, (e) maintenance, and (f) termination. For example, if the members of your target population desire change and in fact have taken some steps toward that change, then the intervention may easily move them into the action phase and beyond. If however, they have not considered change, you may need a significant amount of time and effort to lay the groundwork to prepare them for the change.

The above examples provide you with only a small sample of what can be learned through the existing research on health, psychology, and social issues. This knowledge base will help you articulate a theory of change model for your particular issue area. As a final note to this section, we want to alert you to the fact that it is possible to identify community needs that the community is not yet ready to address. Your ability to assess community readiness for the particular project you design will be crucial to your success. For example, when researchers revealed that HIV is transmitted through the practice of sharing needles to administer intravenous drugs, program developers suggested that the government should provide clean needles to addicts. So many people reacted negatively to this idea that it was rejected in most cities across the United States. This is an extreme yet useful example. People have to be ready for what you want to offer. Similarly, antilittering, antipollution, and recycling legislation would never have passed if the public had not been conscious of the need to protect the environment. Keeping this principle in mind when designing a program is helpful. The goal you hope to achieve requires reaching a certain critical mass of support in the community. The objectives you use to reach the goal are waystations on the road to that goal. The objectives must be acceptable and appropriate to the current thinking in the community.

There are many ways to build programs. These strategies are referred to as *service delivery models.* Most programs are designed to include both direct services and indirect services. Examples of direct services are education, counseling, mentoring, and case management. Examples of indirect services are evaluation, data management, and materials development. You can see from these examples that the term *direct services* implies client contact during service delivery. (Client contact may occur in evaluation through interviews or focus groups, but the evaluation is still considered an indirect service because no service is being delivered to the client.)

CONCEPTUALIZING PROGRAM IDEAS

The previous information in this chapter helped you to think about developing a program with the client or program recipient foremost in your mind. It also challenged you to look to the scientific and professional practice literature to expand your range of good program ideas. Below, we outline a nine-step process to help you to develop your agency's or collaborative's program. Once completed, this process will provide you with the foundation for the full proposal.

1. *Understand the Need/Problem.* Answer the following questions: What is the problem? Why is this a problem? Who is experiencing the problem? What factors contribute to the need/problem?

2. *Brainstorm Solutions.* Think creatively and freely about what might be done to address this problem. Dream of what might be possible and effective in creating change and positive results. Consider the strengths and resources within your target population and the community that can be combined to achieve positive results.

3. *Select Solutions.* Identify your theoretical perspective, and choose the best program ideas from your list. Develop a succinct statement of your theory of change.

4. *Describe Expected Results and Benefits.* What will be the result of the program from the program recipients' perspective (both short and long term)? How will the community benefit?

5. *Think About Barriers.* What will keep this program from being successful? Is the agency prepared to deliver these services? Are there any broader service delivery barriers, such as regulations related to sharing client information? Can you find a way to solve these problems? Would linkage to other agencies address these barriers?

6. *Determine Tasks to Accomplish Solutions.* What are the major activities needed to implement the program—for example, contacts to schedule, staffing, curriculum development, and site procurement?

7. *Estimate Resources Needed.* These are resources in both human and monetary terms. What kind of skills will be needed to implement this project? What will it cost? What other groups need to be involved? Are resources sufficient to achieve the desired outcomes? What are the community's assets or strengths?

8. *Make Necessary Adjustments to Solutions and Benefits.* Most of the time, we think of programs that cost more than available funding, or we find an insurmountable barrier or other problem in implementation. We have to make some adjustments in the project.

9. *Identify Measurement of Outcomes.* How we will measure success? What evidence is needed to determine whether we have been successful? (We will address this aspect of proposal writing in Chapter 6.)

IN SUMMARY: AN EXAMPLE

The following illustrates how program development, theoretical orientations, and service delivery strategies come together. Let's say that I want to design a teen pregnancy prevention program for young adolescents. I am aware that this is a developmental period in which peers have a significant influence upon my client. In the professional literature, I find that social learning theory is effective in addressing peer pressure and social norms. I select a curriculum developed on the principles of social learning theory, and I design my program to include traditional classroom instruction, a teen theater component, a parent education component to improve parent-child communication, and a community advocacy component to address social norms promulgated through advertising and the media.

Then, as I am reading the program evaluation literature, I can find the types of activities that have been used in the past and their success in reaching their goals. For example, I might learn that the classroom educational component is more effective when provided by college-age adults rather than by teens or older adults; consequently, I might choose to design my educational intervention using college-age students. In this case, I can be said to be following "best practices" in that I am combining a sound theoretical orientation with a proven service delivery plan. I am now most likely to succeed.

SUSTAINABILITY AND TRANSFERABILITY

A funder may ask, "Do you plan to continue this project in the future? If so, how do you plan to fund it?" In the majority of cases, the answer to the first question will be "yes," followed by a brief description of how the program may be developed in the future, what major changes may occur in program format, or what new opportunities may be on the horizon. The answer to the second question may be more problematic for the grantwriter. Human nature being what it is, we are likely to have fixed our minds on obtaining the initial funding for the project and not to have concerned ourselves with the funding of the project beyond the current request.

If you view the question from the funder's perspective, you will realize its wisdom. It is nice to support projects that will do wonderful things over the course of the funding, but it is rather frustrating to find that they simply cease when your funds are no longer available. From a funding perspective, it is reasonable to look for projects that have the potential to continue the work into the future.

The following discussion will lead you into planning for the future of your program. Do not be surprised if, again, this process reshapes the project in its current form and leads you to emphasize certain aspects of the project over others.

DETERMINING INCOME-GENERATING POTENTIALS

In reality, most human service programs have the potential to generate some income through the services they provide. However, as many clients are unable to pay the full cost of services rendered, future funding plans often combine the income that can be generated for services and materials with some combination of new grants and contracts. Ask yourself the following questions to ascertain if the project has the potential to generate some income on its own:

- Can you charge a fee for service to your clients?
- Is it possible to market products or materials developed under the project?
- Can you ask your program recipients for a donation?

INSTITUTIONALIZATION OF THE PROJECT

It is extremely useful to consider ways to "institutionalize" your project: that is, to embed it in existing service delivery systems so that it continues after you have completed the contract. For example, we had a contract from the state to provide an educational program at the middle school level. We trained the teachers at the school sites to deliver the program. The program had the potential to continue into the future sustained by revenue received from the schools to continue to train their teachers.

THE LIFE CYCLE OF A PROJECT

What happens when you forecast the project over a 5-year period? This perspective is useful for seeing as yet unrecognized potential for the project. Consider the project as having three stages:

1. There is total reliance on public and private funds as you develop and implement the project.
2. You receive some income as a result of implementing a fee-for-service structure, some grant money, and some donations of both volunteer services and products. You are also selling some of the products and materials developed by the project in the first 1 to 2 years.
3. By the end of the 5 years, the project has enough income coming in to enable at least a small-scale program to continue.

MULTISOURCE FUNDING

Consider if perhaps there is a way to tie the service into other markets over the course of the funding so as to develop a future for the project. For example, the program you are delivering may also meet the needs of individuals in the workplace. You may develop contracts with corporations over the course of the contract that will maintain services in the future. In other words, you will charge the corporations full fee for the services and be able to use this income to subsidize low-income clients.

There may be some opportunity to seek corporate advertising donations to support your project, especially if the company has an interest in reaching a particular target group. You might include a corporate sponsorship in a newsletter, on materials developed for community use, or on an agency home page. The steps you take to ensure the continuance of your project will pay off significantly. You will want to write the answers to these questions with optimism for the future and with creativity. In fact, what you plan for the future just may come true!

4

WRITING THE NEEDS OR PROBLEM STATEMENT

Chapter Highlights

♦ Definitions
♦ The Purpose of the Needs Statement
♦ A Guide to Writing the Needs Statement

DEFINITIONS

The term *needs statement* is generally used in seeking funding for programs or services, whereas *problem statement* usually applies to research-oriented proposals. Often the terms are used interchangeably. For our purposes, we will use the term *needs statement* because our primary focus is on proposals written to improve conditions or address a problem existing within your community.

As outlined in Chapter 3, you begin the proposal development process with an understanding of the need or problem as the basis for conceptualizing your proposed program or intervention. Likewise, when you begin writing the proposal, the needs statement is typically the first section completed. It provides a convincing case regarding the extent and magnitude of the need or problem in your community, and it describes the problem in terms of how people directly or indirectly experience it.

THE PURPOSE OF THE NEEDS
OR PROBLEM STATEMENT

The purpose of the needs statement is to identify the compelling conditions, problems, or issues that are leading you to propose a plan of action. This section of your proposal does *not* describe your approach to address the need or problem; rather, it provides a strong rationale for *why* support should be provided. The needs statement is rooted in factual information. The conceptualization of your proposal is guided by an understanding of the needs or problems not only at the level at which you provide services but also in the larger context of the community, state, or nation.

An effective needs statement does four things:

1. It uses supportive evidence to describe clearly the nature and extent of the need/problem facing those you plan to serve.
2. It illuminates the factors contributing to the problem or the circumstances creating the need.
3. It identifies current gaps in services or programs.
4. Where applicable, it provides a rationale for the transferability of the "promising approaches" or "best practices" you are now proposing.

The needs statement makes clear what is occurring that requires prompt attention before conditions worsen, provides an explanation as to why the problem or need exists, and identifies some of the strategies used in other settings that have the potential for addressing the problem or need in your area. You must thoroughly understand the significance of the needs section, as it provides the underpinnings of the remainder of the proposal. As stated before, the needs section is not the place in the proposal to propose your particular "solution" or project. Rather, it lays the foundation for your particular solution to emerge as one that is responsive to the need.

The needs statement provides an understanding of the impact of the problem not only on those directly affected but also on others, including the community as a whole. A compelling case should be made as to the possible effect of continued *nonintervention* on the individuals, families, and the community at large. One way to make this case is to contrast the costs of prevention or timely intervention to ongoing costs of not addressing the problem. In addition, you can consider emotional and psychological costs related to quality-of-life issues for the program participants and for the community.

Ideally, the needs statement is comprehensive in its treatment of the need/problem but is not boring. Be judicious in your selection of data, and use data that most pointedly tell the story of those you intend to serve. Through the use of data, you want to

1. Demonstrate that you have a thorough understanding of the problem and those you seek to serve.
2. Demonstrate that you are knowledgeable about the types of interventions that are successful in addressing this problem for your client base.
3. Indicate that you are aware of possible barriers to the provision of service to this population.
4. Demonstrate that the problem you are addressing is the same issue that the funder wants to address.
5. Lay the groundwork to lead the funder to the conclusion that your approach is "client centered" and obviously one of the best possible choices to address this problem.

A GUIDE TO WRITING THE NEEDS
OR PROBLEM STATEMENT

Obviously, you cannot use all of the information that you find. Scrutinize it carefully to make the best possible case for your proposal. At this point in the process, many grantwriters face the mountains of data in front of them with increasing anxiety. The problem now becomes one of condensing and editing the data to make a powerful statement in a limited number of pages.

To help you organize the information and begin writing, we will now break down the needs statement into four sections (drawing on the conceptual framework presented in Chapter 3). (This is only a template to help you organize and is not meant to be your final version of the document. The examples we are using are based on hypothetical data—in other words, data made up for illustrative purposes only.)

SECTION 1: THE NATURE AND EXTENT OF THE NEED/PROBLEM

This section could be subtitled "What is the need/problem, and who is experiencing it?" In it, you will try to provide a clear picture of the incidence of the problem (e.g., the number of people per thousand in the population who experience the problem and the rates by ethnicity, gender, age, and educational level).

In this example, we begin with a factual opening sentence that states the topic and captures the attention of the reader. We begin to define the problem and give a percentage of the total population who experience homelessness in the geographical area to be served:

> The majority of families are only one paycheck away from homelessness, and for (number of people) in (your local geographic area), this fact is all too real. The majority of the homeless (defined as those without semipermanent or permanent shelter) in (your county) are single mothers with children representing the fastest-growing segment of the homeless population.

The next step is to compare the local-level data to the state and national data. If the incidence of the problem is greater than the state or national rates, your job is easy, and your next sentence might sound like this:

> In fact, in (year) the homelessness rate in (your county) was _____, which exceeded the state rate of ____ and the national rate of _____ in the same year (source of data).

If your rate is lower than the state and national rates, study the data and see if there is a significant change in the rate in your own county from the past, and you may be able to say something like this:

> Although lower than the state and national rates of ____ and ____ respectively, (your county) has seen a significant increase in homelessness over the past 5 years and, without intervention, will meet and exceed national rates within the next ___ years (source of data).

If your rate is so low as to make your application noncompetitive, you may need to find some unique reason why your community's problem is significant. For example, you may have higher crime rates as a result of homelessness, or you may have more health problems within the homeless population. Contrast the high incidence of the problem to the low incidence of homelessness to make a stronger case.

In the next paragraph, we address the issues of ethnicity, education, and length of time of homelessness:

> In (your county), the rate of homelessness by ethnicity is ____% white, ____% Latino. ____% African American, and ____% Asian. The rate for (ethnic group) is proportionately higher than all others. The average educational level for homeless people is ___ years of schooling, but even individuals with college degrees can be, at some point in time, homeless. The average length of time that individuals are homeless is ____ months.

You will notice that we have not made a highly emotional appeal to the funder but have already put a face on the client in the first paragraph. We feel that the funder, as well as the human service provider, is all too aware of the personal toll these problems bring. Overdramatizing the problem can work to your disadvantage.

In the above example, the data are effectively presented within the context of the community. When you place data in relationship to other data (e.g., state or national level) or other associated problems, you strengthen your request and increase the sense of urgency. (Note below how effective the word *only* is when using comparative data.) For example, compare the following two statements:

> Fifty percent of the young people in the county do not graduate from high school.

versus

> Fifty percent of the young people in the county do not graduate from high school, whereas the dropout rate is only 10% in the state and 27% nationally.

SECTION 2: FACTORS CONTRIBUTING TO THE PROBLEM OR CONDITIONS

In this section of the proposal, you will address the causes of the problem/the needs of the clients. These may include

1. A lack of skill, knowledge, or awareness
2. Debilitating attitudes or harmful values
3. Physical or mental challenges and limitations
4. Dysfunctional or problem behavior
5. Limited resources or access to services
6. Institutional and systemic barriers, including fragmented services
7. Policies, practices, or laws that have negative consequences (either intended or unintended)

In this section, you want to account for each of the factors that cause the problem you are addressing. The following paragraph begins this task:

> A variety of conditions may ultimately lead to homelessness. Of the homeless population, ___% are mentally ill and unemployed; ___% have experienced the loss of a job; ___% have recently divorced; and ___% are addicted

to drugs or alcohol (source of data, year). The top reason for job loss in the past year was personal health problems, including depression, followed by poor work performance, a lack of job-related skills, absenteeism, and health problems with other family members. In most cases, homelessness does not happen all at once. The family uses all available resources to maintain housing and often has 1 to 3 months of financial struggle before ending up on the streets.

A discussion of barriers to resolving this problem can also be included in this section. For example, the stigma associated with homelessness may be so great as to cause people to delay seeking assistance, or the clients themselves may have attitudes or beliefs that prevent them from benefiting from assistance.

Each of the "causes" of the problem stated in the above example is significant for program planning and can be further explored along socioeconomic and cultural lines if necessary. The second paragraph, which indicates that homelessness is a process, is laying some of the groundwork necessary to support our project—early intervention to prevent impending homelessness—but of course, we won't say anything about that in this section.

Finally, we want to warn you about one of the most common mistakes we see in this section of the proposal: what is known as *circular reasoning* (Kiritz, 1980). Circular reasoning occurs when one argues that the problem is the lack of the service that one is proposing. For example, you might write in the needs statement that "the problem facing many teens is that they do not have access to a teen peer support group" and proceed merrily on your way to proposing teen support groups as a solution to the problem. The above statement, however, has failed to identify the problems of teenagers that can be addressed through a peer support group (e.g., loneliness, isolation, depression); in fact, it gives the idea that the absence of a teen support group is the problem! Consider the way in which the following paragraph might better address the role of peer support groups in addressing a need:

An adolescent spends an average of ____ hours per day in contact with other teens in school and after-school activities. Research indicates that teens obtain approximately ____% of their information on drugs, sexuality, and health-related topics from their peers (source of data, year). From a developmental perspective, teens are moving away from parental and other adult authority and toward developing their own personal authority. In this process, teens attach to and relate best to their peers.

SECTION 3: IMPACT OF THE NEED/PROBLEM

In this section, you want to look at the impact of the problem on the client, the client's family, and the community at large and the benefits to be derived through intervention, treatment, or prevention of the problem. The following paragraph begins this process:

> The problem of homelessness exacts a significant toll on the homeless person and family. Children who are homeless are often uprooted from their schools and their friends, suffer from poor nutrition, and lack even the most basic of preventive care services, such as immunizations. If one is a homeless adult, one has no address or phone number to use to obtain employment.
>
> Once an individual is homeless, the demands on community resources are great. The Government Accounting Office has estimated that it costs tax-payers approximated $35,000 per homeless family per year to provide for the family's basic needs. In a study by (source, year), it was shown that timely intervention targeted at a family in crisis costs approximately $15,000 per year, a savings of over half the cost of delayed intervention! The intervention resulted not only in significant financial savings but also in fewer days lost from school and improved health outcomes among home-less children.

As you may have guessed, we are continuing to lay the groundwork for our early intervention project in response to the problem of homelessness. We want to show that our proposed project is cost-effective and that it reduces the negative consequences associated with homelessness. But we won't say anything about the proposed project in this section either.

SECTION 4: PROMISING APPROACHES
FOR IMPROVED RESULTS

In this section, you can discuss the theoretical perspectives that have proven to be useful in designing interventions, successful approaches used in other geographic areas, and, typically, the barriers to resolving the problem. For example, you might begin like this:

> Several promising strategies have been developed to address the problem of homelessness. The first is the Homeless Project based in Seattle, Washington (source of data, year). This project targeted a subset of homeless drug-abusing adults and offered treatment incentives and comprehensive services. The program helped over 67% of its participants kick the drug habit, and after a year, 87% of those were employed and paying for their own housing.

Other projects have been extremely successful in helping individuals in crisis avoid homelessness altogether. One project, in Michigan, opened a one-stop service center for struggling families. Through a combination of debt counseling, psychological services, educational remediation, job training, and health services, a full 90% of clients maintained their homes. In addition, this approach has the advantage of avoiding public resistance to a homeless shelter in the community.

In this section of the needs statement, you are referencing the particular theoretical and practical program components that will be effective in addressing the need/problem. Discuss the pros and cons of particular strategies, and consider the unique needs of your participants. If a collaborative approach is planned, identify the advantages of this strategy over a single organizational approach. This section provides a rationale for the methods section, which will be discussed in Chapter 5.

5

WRITING GOALS, OBJECTIVES, AND IMPLEMENTATION ACTIVITIES

Chapter Highlights

- ♦ Program Goals
- ♦ Formulating Objectives
- ♦ Developing the Implementation Plan
- ♦ Writing the Project Narrative

Understanding the needs or problems in your community and the capacity to address them leads to the development of goals, objectives, and a plan of action. This chapter will distinguish among these terms and provide guidelines for developing these sections of the proposal. The next chapter will describe evaluation methods for determining whether your objectives were achieved.

Table 5.1 refines the conceptual framework discussed earlier in Chapter 3 to show the connections among the sections of the proposal and identifies the questions each should answer.

PROGRAM GOALS

The two terms *goals* and *objectives* are often used interchangeably. For our purposes, we are distinguishing between them. *Goals* respond to identified needs or problems and are statements of the ultimate mission or purpose of the program or collaborative. They represent an ideal or "hoped-for" state of the desired change. *Objectives* represent the immediate desired and measurable outcomes or results that are essential for

TABLE 5.1   Conceptual Framework for Writing Goals and Objectives

Determine the Problem/Need
   What is the problem/need?
   What are the conditions or circumstances that need to be addressed?
   Who experiences or is affected by them?
   What are the factors contributing to their occurrence?

State the Goal(s)
   What is the *ultimate* desired result for changing conditions or circumstances?
   What are the agreed-on issues/needs to be addressed in the long run?

State the Objectives
   What will be the *immediate* outcomes, results, or benefits?
   What changes are expected during a specified time period that will address the
      problem/need?

Describe the Implementation Plan
   What activities or actions will be taken to lead to the desired results?
   What is the theory of practice that will achieve the expected outcomes?

Develop a Plan for Measuring the Expected Outcomes
   What are the short- and long-term indicators toward achieving the outcomes?
   What data will be collected to determine the extent to which the outcomes were
      achieved?

---

achieving the ultimate goals. The goal of a program may be "to eliminate child abuse" or "to prevent domestic violence." The objective may be "to improve family functioning by 25%" or "to decrease by 10% the cases of reported domestic violence in Grant City."

Most proposals identify one, two or, at the most, three goals. Other examples of goals are

- To provide a pollution-free environment in the United States
- To ensure that all pregnant women in the state of California receive early and adequate prenatal care
- To eliminate birth defects in Grant County

As you see in these examples, goals are ambitious statements! They are the desired state of things. As such, they are not generally attainable over the short term, yet they help us to keep our focus and communicate the project clearly to others.

Goals are usually written indicating the geographic area in which the services are to be provided. To write the goals, return to the needs or problems you seek to address, and state the major reasons for your work. The following questions can assist you in developing goals:

1. What ideal condition will exist if we eliminate, prevent, or improve the situation?
2. What is the overall, long-term condition desired for our program recipients?

In some cases, the funders may provide the goals associated with the funding. For example, if you are applying for funding through federal or state sources, the goals are usually listed in the Request for Proposals, in which case it is advisable to simply restate those goals, adding the geographic area of service. If you are developing both goals and objectives, double-check to be sure that the goals fit within legislative mandates or other funding missions.

FORMULATING OBJECTIVES

Objectives are the *expected* results of the actions taken to attain the goal. They provide the "promise" of what will be achieved over the course of the funding period. Objectives are specific, achievable, measurable statements about what is going to be accomplished within a certain time frame. Typically, three to four objectives are derived from each goal and are defined more narrowly because you are predicting that you will accomplish certain things within an agreed-on time period. It is wise to develop objectives for each type of change expected and for each target group. For example, with the goal "to eliminate child abuse and neglect," some objectives may be targeted at parents, some at teachers, and some at the community at large.

In collaboration, agencies can develop objectives that are agency specific or shared with collaborative partners. Developing shared objectives within a collaborative can be especially challenging because organizations must collectively take responsibility for the desired results. Shared objectives require a certain level of trust between agencies because the objective must be met for reimbursement to occur.

TYPES OF OBJECTIVES

The two major types of objectives, process and outcome, are explained below.

Process Objectives

Process objectives (a) describe the expected improvements in the operations or procedures, (b) quantify the expected change in the usage of services or methods, or (c) identify how much service will be received. Process objectives do not indicate the impact on the program recipients; rather, they are formulated because the activities involved in implementation are important to the overall understanding of how a problem or need gets addressed. They help to provide insight into experimental, unique, and innovative approaches or techniques used in a program. Process objectives are usually designed to increase knowledge about how to improve the delivery of services.

For example, process objectives might be written for different types and amounts of staff interaction with clients, to examine outreach activities with difficult-to-reach youth, or to describe interagency collaboration. A process objective focused on coalition building is not concerned with *what* is accomplished by the coalition but with *how* the coalition is formed and maintained. Process objectives may be written to study program implementation methodology or to address the internal functioning and structure of an organization, as in the following objectives.

- Ten child abuse prevention support groups will be formed by agency staff within the first 6 months of the project.
- A computerized client charting system will be developed to track and retrieve 50% of client records by June 30, 20xx.

Both examples focus on the activities required to provide service rather than the impact of those activities on the clients or participants. Process objectives are not routinely developed in proposals because funders typically focus on giving funds for the direct benefit of the program recipients.

Outcome Objectives

The second and more common type of objective is known as an outcome objective. In contrast to process objectives, outcome objectives are used to describe the expected benefits to program recipients. An outcome objective specifies a target group and identifies what will happen to them as a result of the intervention or approach. Outcomes may depict a change in one or more levels, such as client, program, agency, system, cross-systems, or community (Gardner, 1999). They indicate the effectiveness of the approach used by stating what will be different. Changes may occur in multiple areas such as

- Improved behavior
- Increased skills

- Changed attitudes, values, or beliefs
- Increased knowledge or awareness
- Improved conditions
- Elimination of institutional or systemic barriers
- More effective policies, practices, or laws

Well-stated outcome objectives provide the following:

- A time frame
- The target group (possibly identified in terms of their age, gender, and ethnicity, if applicable)
- The number of program recipients
- The expected measurable results or benefits
- The geographic location or service locale such as a group home, hospital, jail, or neighborhood (may be stated in the goal)

Objectives use action verbs (*reduce, increase, decrease, promote, demonstrate*) to indicate the expected direction of the change in knowledge, attitude, behavior, skills, or conditions. They define the topic area to be measured (e.g., self-esteem, nutrition, communication) and the date by which the results will be accomplished.

As you develop outcome objectives, think again about the needs of the program recipients and the community. Is the purpose of your program or collaborative to increase knowledge about certain topics so as to affect behavior? Do they have the knowledge but still persist in unhealthy behavior, leading you to work more directly on attitudes, values, or beliefs? What exactly do you hope to change? Will you focus on improving the conditions for a group? The objective should capture the primary purpose of the service you provide.

Often, staff in therapeutic settings have difficulty in formulating measurable outcome objectives and are more apt to develop process objectives. Their difficulty lies in finding ways to conceptualize and make observable the progress of clients, especially those who are in non-behaviorally-oriented counseling settings, and in subjecting the client to a formal evaluation process. Thus, staff often find it easier to describe the therapeutic process as an objective, without stating a quantifiable or measurable outcome objective.

However, as funders focus greater attention on results-based accountability and efficient allocation of resources through such mechanisms as purchase of service contracts, agencies will need to increase their capacity to measure their effectiveness and impact. Having an in-depth understanding of the nature of the need/problem and the factors associated with its occurrence, along with formulating a well-developed theory of change that identifies progressive indicators or benchmarks toward the desired change, can help guide the development of outcome objectives. Too often, outcomes are aimed at changing complex or chronic conditions within a short time period and are not rooted in a full understanding of what it will actually take to achieve those desired changes.

Furthermore, an organization's theory of change may not incorporate important factors that contribute to the occurrence of the problem. For example, the goal may be to reduce child abuse and neglect, and the outcome may be to improve family functioning by increasing knowledge about effective parenting. At the same time, alcohol and drug abuse may be mediating factors working against improved family functioning that are not being addressed. Thus, "increasing knowledge" may be necessary for change but may not be sufficient to achieve the stated outcome objective of improved family functioning.

One way for organizations to address this is to partner with other groups. A progression of outcomes is developed that identifies the change or benefits toward an overall desired end. The United Way of America (1996) described three levels of outcomes:

1. *Initial outcomes*: the first benefits or changes that participants experience (e.g., changes in knowledge, attitudes, or skills). They are not the end in themselves and may not be especially meaningful in terms of the quality of participants' lives. They are necessary steps toward the desired end and therefore are important indicators of participants' progress toward those ends.

2. *Intermediate outcomes*: often the changes in behavior that result from new knowledge, attitudes, or skills.

3. *Longer term outcomes*: the ultimate outcomes that a program desires to achieve for its participants. They represent meaningful changes for participants, often in their condition or status. (p. 32)

The following is an example of a short-term outcome objective focused on increased knowledge of the target group: "Two hundred pregnant women living in the Grant neighborhood will increase their knowledge about prenatal care by 40% by June 30, 20xx." A longer term outcome could be stated as "Eighty percent of the pregnant women living in the Grant neighborhood will access prenatal care in the first trimester by June 30, 20xx."

The beginning grantwriter is apt to confuse an objective with an implementation activity. A common error is to state the actual program or service that is going to be offered without indicating its benefits. Such an error would result in the following example of a *poor* objective: "One thousand youths between the ages of 12 and 16 will participate in a 6-week education program on violence prevention by June 30, 20xx." In this example, the "6-week education program" is an implementation activity. The following questions may help the writer to reach the outcome level of the objective: Why are youths receiving a 6-week program? To increase their knowledge or improve their skills? To change behavior? A revised, "good" objective could look like this: "One thousand youths between the ages of 12 and 16 will increase their knowledge by 30% in conflict resolution and anger management by June 30, 20xx." As you write your objectives, make sure you are stating the expected *outcome,* or changes in the program recipients, and not just identifying the approach being used.

In summary, the following example shows how a single goal can lead to several process and outcome objectives:

Sample Goal: To prevent drug use among young people by promoting their academic success and emotional well-being.

Process Objectives:

1. To form a coalition of 10 youth-serving agencies in order to develop a comprehensive plan for providing after-school activities at two junior high schools by June 30, 20xx.
2. To establish a multilingual teen drug prevention hotline with a corps of 100 volunteer high school students by June 30, 20xx.
3. To develop a multimedia drug abuse prevention campaign targeted to junior high school students and their parents by June 30, 20xx.

Outcome Objectives:

4. One hundred at-risk junior high school students attending the after-school peer counseling program will increase by 60% their knowledge about the dangers of drug and alcohol use by June 30, 20xx.
5. One hundred and twenty-five junior high school students who are academically at risk will show a 30% improvement in their reading and math scores by June 30, 20xx.
6. One hundred and fifty parents will increase by 60% their knowledge about effective communication techniques for teaching their children

about decision making, goal setting, and the dangers and lure of drugs by
June 30, 20xx.

7. One hundred parents will increase their involvement with their children's
   school by 10% by June 30, 20xx.

Appropriately, the goal statement provides a general aim and direction
for the project but lacks specificity as to what will be achieved. The process
objectives identify the approach to be used but do *not* state what impact it
will have on the participants. (It is not necessary for every proposal to have
both process and outcome objectives. Process objectives are written when
the funder has indicated that the desired outcome is to develop a new
approach or test out a particular method of service delivery.) The outcome
objectives specify "who" and "how many" are to achieve "what results."

Common errors in writing objectives include (a) putting more than one
measurable outcome in the objective and (b) saying much more than is
needed in the objective. Keep the objectives simple and clear. Though you
want to "stretch" as far as possible with a vision for improved conditions
or circumstances, objectives should be realistic and not promise more than
can be delivered within the time period stated. Remember also that objectives are directly tied to the contractual relationship between the agency
and the funder and that consequently the agency may be held accountable
if the objective is not met.

DEVELOPING THE IMPLEMENTATION PLAN

The implementation plan is the "nuts and bolts" of the proposal: It provides a clear account of what you plan to do, who will do it, and in what
time frame the activities will be accomplished. This section is the logical
next step after writing the goals and objectives, for it explains to the funder
how the objectives will be achieved. It presents a reasonable and coherent
action plan that justifies the resources requested. The design of your program should generate confidence that it reflects sound decision making
and is the most feasible approach for addressing the need/problem. This
section will assist you in formulating a step-by-step implementation plan.

The program objectives serve as the foundation for developing the
implementation plan. The tasks and activities link directly to accomplishing the objectives and provide the funder with an indication of the reason-
ableness and rationality of your implementation plan for achieving the
desired results.

PREPARATORY ACTIVITIES

A variety of activities and resources will be needed to achieve program outcomes. The resources include personnel (e.g., staff, volunteers, program recipients, community groups, other organizations), nonpersonnel (e.g., equipment, facilities, materials, supplies), and other funds needed. (One must also take into consideration any constraints on the program, such as policies and regulations that affect the utilization of the resources.)

Preparatory activities are the start-up activities or general tasks necessary to get the program underway. With each task, it is also useful to identify the person responsible for accomplishing the activity and to estimate the time needed for completion. Although the type of preparatory activities will vary depending on the nature of your program, the following are typical and are not listed in any time sequence:

- Developing staffing plans
- Selecting site/facilities
- Ordering special equipment
- Selecting or developing program products or materials
- Setting up interagency agreements and collaboration plans
- Building community linkages and partnerships
- Developing outreach strategies and approaches to involving program participants
- Setting up evaluation mechanisms

PROGRAM-RELATED ACTIVITIES

In general, human services programming can be grouped into five major categories: (a) training or education, (b) information development and dissemination, (c) counseling and other support services, (d) provision of resources or changing conditions, and (e) advocacy and systems change. Remember that program design must be considerate of the diversity that exists within the target population. The following questions are designed to assist you in identifying the kinds of activities that might be required to conduct programs in the five major categories:

1. Training or education programs (e.g., career development workshop, job preparation training, parent education)

   - What are the training or educational objectives?
   - What will be the content of the presentation(s)?

- What strategies or techniques (e.g., teaching aids and tools) will be most effective with the population?
- Who will conduct the training? What criteria will be used to select trainers?
- What will be the typical format and schedule? Does it take into consideration the program participants' needs and schedules?
- What other arrangements will be needed for the program participants to fully participate?

2. Information development and dissemination (e.g., ad campaign for drug abuse prevention, videotape on AIDS prevention, health care newsletter, parent training manual, resource and referral service)

- Who is the targeted audience?
- What will be the content and format?
- How will it be developed? Who will develop it?
- Which group(s) will review before distribution to determine effectiveness and appropriateness?
- What dissemination strategies will be used?

3. Counseling and other support services (e.g., bereavement counseling, support group for victims of abuse and violence, drug and alcohol abuse counseling, and crisis hotline)

- What counseling strategies or techniques will be used?
- What are the underlying assumptions or evidence of the validity of the techniques with the specific population?
- What will be the counseling process and format?
- What issues and content will be addressed?
- What other resources (e.g., support system, professionals) will be needed by the program participants?
- What are the plans to reduce the attrition rate?

4. Provision of resources or changing conditions (e.g., transportation for the disabled, meals program for older Americans, youth recreation program, health care screening)

- What resources will be provided?
- What is the most effective delivery approach for the population?
- When, where, and how will resources be delivered?

- Who will develop, organize, and deliver them?
- Are any special equipment and/or materials needed? How will these be obtained?

5. Advocacy and systems change (e.g., legislation to ban smoking in public places, welfare reform, health care coverage for low-income families, alcohol and drug treatment on demand)

- What are the research and data on the issues?
- What are the policies, regulations, or laws that need to be changed?
- What coalitions or partnerships are necessary to achieve the changes?
- What are the most effective strategies for effective change? What are important media strategies?
- What compromises are acceptable?
- Who will be the spokespersons?

UNITS OF SERVICE

Often referred to as the "output" of your program, units of service describe the types or amounts of service provided and thus relate to the volume of work that is expected or the products of your program. Examples are "100 hours of group counseling with 75 drug abuse addicts," "200 health care newsletters printed and distributed to persons 55 years and older," and "150 high school dropouts attending 10 computer training sessions."

The results or outcomes are influenced by how well the program has been conceptualized and whether there were sufficient units of service to achieve the objective. For example, the "output" of the program might be that 75 drug abuse addicts received 100 hours of group counseling, but the benefit or result would be whether and how long the participants remained drug-free.

WRITING THE PROJECT NARRATIVE

This section may also be referred to in the proposal guidelines as the "Project Description." Included in it (again, usually) are subsections called "Scope of Work," "Methods," or "Program Approach." Often, grantwriters are unclear as to how to proceed with the writing of this section, as proposal instructions may lack specific details about the content and format.

In our experience, if there are incomplete instructions, we complete the narrative section by providing a complete explanation of the project, starting with the goals of the project, followed by the first objective, its implementation activities, and a detailed description of the evaluation method, and continuing forward objective by objective in the above manner. It is possible to bring more detail into the narrative section, including the rationale for particular program selection and staffing, for example, than into any other section of the proposal.

The following is an example of a project narrative:

> The Learning for Life Project has two goals: to ensure that all children receive a quality education and to eliminate school dropouts. The first objective under Goal No. 1 states: "Objective 1.1: Two hundred (200) school-age children will improve their grades by 20% by June 30, 20xx." To accomplish this objective, each of the 200 children will have his or her educational needs assessed by a learning specialist and be matched with a tutor who has the necessary skills to help the child. In the first month of the project, the Project Director and the Learning Specialist will select appropriate assessment instruments for the children. Relationships currently exist with the University of Grant State and Grant City College to develop the tutoring pool. Faculty in the School of Education at these universities will assess student abilities, and the tutors will be ready to be matched by the second month of the project. Over the academic year the tutors will spend approximately 100 hours with each of their students during the regular school day. The evaluation of this objective will be accomplished by assessing student grade point average at the start of tutoring based on grades of the previous quarter and compared to the grades of the quarter ending after the completion of tutoring. If students demonstrated an improvement in their grades by one full level, the objective will be met. The Project Director will be responsible to oversee the implementation of the evaluation component.
>
> Objective 1.2 states: "Two hundred parents of children in tutoring will increase their time spent providing homework assistance by 10% by June 30, 20xx."

(The writer will continue to address the implementation activities and the evaluation for this objective and then address all the other goals and objectives of the project.)

It is not unusual to be required to complete other subsections to the narrative, including Scope of Work forms, a time line, and possibly some other visual representation of the project. Experienced grantwriters appreciate the opportunity to present the project activities in a variety of formats to ensure that the reviewers have a complete understanding of how the objectives will be achieved. In addition, computer-generated charts, figures, and project flow diagrams (see Schaefer, 1985, 1987) are often used to enhance the presentation.

SCOPE OF WORK

As stated above, many state agencies require a Scope of Work form (Table 5.2), which provides the basis for the legal contract. This format shows the relationship between the goal, the objectives, the activities, and staff responsible for the activities; a time line; and the evaluation. Of course, this is somewhat redundant to the narrative, but it does offer the advantage of a quick, one-page synopsis of each objective, implementation activity (approach), time line, and evaluation. In Table 5.2, we have filled out a Scope of Work form using the above example.

As you study the Scope of Work form, you will notice that the goal is written across the top of the page and is numbered (e.g., Goal No. 1). The first column contains an objective that is numbered in sequence relative to the goal for which it applies. The second column identifies the major activities that will accomplish the particular objective. It is also customary to list, underneath each activity, the job title of the individual(s) responsible for that activity. The third column, the time line column, indicates the start and end date for each activity. The final column is for the evaluation of the objective, which identifies how each objective will be measured to determine if it has been achieved.

PROJECT TIMETABLE

In addition to a description of project activities, funders typically desire to see a schedule of those activities. A visual display of the action plan provides the reader with a real sense of when different phases of the project will be undertaken. It also helps to generate confidence in your ability to effectively plan and carry out the grant or contract requirements.

A variety of techniques can be used to present the project's timetable. One of the most common is a GANTT chart, which shows activities in relation to a time dimension (see Table 5.3). In preparing a GANTT chart, (a) list the major activities and tasks, (b) estimate the amount of time to be expended on each activity or task, and (c) determine how the activity is spread across a time period. The time period is typically divided into months or quarters, and an activity's beginning and end points are depicted with row bars, X's, or similar markings. Generally, activities are listed in the order in which they will be accomplished (a forward sequence).

TABLE 5.2 Scope of Work Form

Contractor ___*Geta Grant Agency*___
Contract Number _____
Agency Number _____

County ___*Grant County*___

SCOPE OF WORK

The contractor shall work toward achieving the following goals and will accomplish the following objectives. This shall be done by performing the specified activities and evaluating the results using the listed methods to focus on process and/or outcome.

Goal No. ___*1*___ (specify) ___*To ensure that all children receive a quality education*___

MEASURABLE OBJECTIVE(S)	IMPLEMENTATION ACTIVITIES	TIME LINE	METHODS OF EVALUATING PROCESS AND/OR OUTCOME OF OBJECTIVE(S)
1.1. Two hundred (200) school-age children will improve their grades by 20% by June 30, 20xx.	1.1.A. The educational needs of the students will be assessed. (Learning Specialist, Project Director)	7/1/xx to 11/30/xx	1.1.A. Student grade point averages will be obtained for the quarter prior to tutoring and the quarter following the end of tutoring. If a 20% increase in grades is accomplished, the objective will be met. (Project Director, Learning Specialist)
	1.1.B. Assessment instruments for the children will be reviewed and selected for use. (Learning Specialist)	7/1/xx to 8/31/xx	
	1.1.C. Students will be matched with tutors who will spend approximately 100 hours with each of their students. (Project Director)	10/1/xx to 4/30/xx	
	1.1.D. Student grade point records will be obtained for appropriate quarters to conduct evaluation. (Project Director)	10/1/xx to 6/15/xx	

TABLE 5.3   GANTT Chart, GetaGrant Agency, Learning for Life Project, Fiscal Year 20xx to 20xx

Objective	July	Aug	Sept	Oct	Nov	Dec	Jan	Feb	Mar	Apr	May	June
Obj.1.1. 200 school-age children will improve their grades by 20% by June 30, 20xx												
Identify and select assessment protocols	X	X										
Assess students' learning needs		X	X	X	X							
Faculty assesses tutors' abilities		X	X									
Students and tutors matched			X	X								
Tutoring begins				X	X	X	X	X	X	X		
Pretutoring grades collected from school sites			X	X	X	X	X	X	X	X		
Post-tutoring grades collected						X	X	X	X	X	X	X
Evaluation report						X			X		X	
Obj. 1.2. 200 parents of children in tutoring will increase their time spent providing homework assistance by 10% by June 30, 20xx												
Continue implementation activities												

By examining the GANTT chart, one sees which activities are to occur within a particular time frame, and this can be useful for project monitoring. Also, some funders require quarterly reports, and from the GANTT chart they are able to determine what you plan to accomplish each quarter. It is a good idea to include the preparation of any reports to the funder as an activity on the chart.

If there are few activities or the project has a relatively short time span, the time line format shown in Table 5.4 may be used.

TABLE 5.4   Sample Brief Time Line, Geta Grant Agency, Learning for Life
Project, Fiscal Year 20xx to 20xx

Activity	Time
Hire staff	July 1 to July 30
Train staff	August 1 to September 15
Develop curriculum	July 1 to September 30
Schedule workshops	August 15 to September 30
Conduct workshops	October 1 to May 30
Conduct evaluation	October 1 to May 30
Prepare final report	June 1 to June 25

6

WRITING THE EVALUATION PLAN

Chapter Highlights

- ♦ The Benefits of Evaluation
- ♦ Developing an Evaluation Plan
- ♦ Writing the Evaluation Section
- ♦ Other Evaluation Considerations

THE BENEFITS OF EVALUATION

There are many advantages to having a sound evaluation plan, for it is through the development of effective evaluation strategies that major strides have been made in human service programming. Gone are the days when it was simply sufficient to do "good." Now the need is urgent both to "prove" that good and necessary things are done (outcome evaluation) and to document how they were done (process evaluation). Moreover, the transferability of "best practices" is enhanced when there is supportive evidence that the approaches used are indeed related to positive results.

Evaluation research can be used in assessing the merit of programs, techniques, and program materials. From a broad view, the results of such research can form the basis of position papers for lawmakers as well as the creation of advocacy groups for certain causes. In the grantwriting process, the benefits of evaluation research and data can be viewed from two perspectives: the funder's and the organization's.

From the perspective of the funder, the results of your evaluation may be used to

1. Determine whether the funds were used appropriately and whether the objectives, as stated in the proposal, were accomplished.
2. Assess whether the program's benefits are worth the cost.
3. Assist in the development of future funding objectives addressing the same needs/problem.
4. Promote positive public relations through promotion of the benefits derived through funded projects.

From the perspective of the organization, evaluation has the following benefits:

1. It compels the organization to clarify program objectives so that they are measurable.
2. It helps the agency to continually refine its approaches to service.
3. It provides feedback on the level of effort and cost required to accomplish the tasks so that adjustments may be made in the future.
4. It increases the organization's capacity to meet the need through increased knowledge about the population served and about effective interventions.
5. It assists the organization to communicate benefits of service to the public and thereby to increase public support.
6. It assists other organizations in program development through the dissemination of results.

DEVELOPING AN EVALUATION PLAN

In most human service agencies, evaluation plans are kept fairly simple due to a number of factors, including financial concerns, constraints imposed by the program recipients, the environment of the program, and limited staff expertise in evaluation methodology. When the organization is part of a collaborative, data collection and sharing may be especially challenging. Funders will sometimes provide guidelines on the evaluation design expected, or they may simply state that an assessment of the program's accomplishments is required. Read the Request for Proposals or application instructions carefully to ascertain the nature of the evaluation desired.

When you design an evaluation, remember that you are developing a plan to determine whether the stated objectives were achieved. The objectives represent the "promise," and the evaluation provides evidence that the promise was fulfilled. There are several terms associated with types of evaluations: for example, *impact, product, process, outcome, formative,* and *summative.* In this chapter, we briefly describe the features of a process evaluation but focus more directly on developing a plan to measure your results. Increasingly, staff are expected to provide extensive information about the direct benefits of the program to the participants (or the community). Much is being written about outcomes evaluation, results-based accountability, or impact studies. It is essential that time and resources be invested in embedding programs within a results-focused framework. Process and outcomes evaluations answer different types of questions and, when used in combination, can provide a more complete picture of the way the program was implemented and the extent to which the outcomes were achieved.

GOALS OF A PROCESS EVALUATION

Process evaluation provides an assessment of the procedures used in conducting the program. A primary goal of this type of evaluation is to gather feedback information during the operation of the program to determine whether changes are warranted. The results can also be incorporated to improve the implementation of a subsequent program with a similar focus.

Process evaluation provides an understanding of how you achieved the results: That is, it describes what happened, how the activities were accomplished, and at what level of effort. Conducting this type of evaluation requires close monitoring of the program and may include

1. Assessment of participant satisfaction with the program
2. Detailed tracking of staff efforts
3. Assessment of administrative and programmatic functions and activities
4. A determination of the program's efficiency

Such an assessment can provide information on the level of staff effort necessary to achieve certain program results, the level of outreach necessary to reach clients, and the level of participant satisfaction with the staff, facilities, and/or program. For example, in addition to determining whether there was improvement in family functioning (outcome evaluation), you may also be interested in assessing the effectiveness of different family outreach methods used (process). To undertake this latter evaluation, you would identify the outreach activities that attracted families to your program, such as flyers, public speaking, newspaper articles, directory listings, and referral through other agencies. You might then survey the families to determine which outreach strategies they responded to, as well as measure the level of effort and cost involved with each strategy.

Process evaluation goals may focus on the delivery of a particular service or co-located services of a collaborative or may assess the entire operation. The following is a sample of the kinds of questions with different program foci that may guide you in formulating a process evaluation.

Training or Education Programs

1. What is the content of the training? What are the unique features of the training?
2. How is the training conducted? What procedures, techniques, materials, and products are used? What is the background of the trainer(s)? What costs are associated with the training?
3. What is the background of the individuals trained? Which training techniques are most effective with which groups?
4. What are staff's perceptions of the quality of the training, how it can be improved, and the level of effort required to accomplish each facet of the training?

Products/Materials Development

1. What and how are the products/materials developed and tested?
2. How are the products/materials disseminated?
3. How are the products used, including how often, by whom, and by how many?
4. What are user and staff perceptions about the products/materials?
5. What are the cost savings associated with the products/materials?

Improving Operations or Procedures

1. What is the nature of the improved operations or procedures? How do they contrast with the previous ones?
2. What is the implementation process for the new procedures or operations?
3. How do the new procedures or operations affect service? Contrast cost savings and level of effort between old and new.

Improving Conditions

1. What was the theory of change, and what was the change process?
2. Which techniques/methods are most effective in contributing to improving the conditions?

3. How does the change process affect agency or collaborative operations, including staff roles?
4. What are the cost savings?

GOALS OF AN OUTCOME EVALUATION

An outcome evaluation determines how well the program achieved its objectives. In contrast to a process evaluation, which answers the question "How was the result achieved?" an outcome evaluation focuses on "What and/or how much was achieved?" and "What changes occurred in program participants or community conditions?" Funders are more apt to expect such answers because they are seeking some explanation of what was accomplished with the resources provided. This type of evaluation is sometimes referred to as the "so what" of the program: So what happened, so what was accomplished, so what difference did it make?

An outcome evaluation can range in design from simply assessing what changes occurred in the program participants that are attributable to the program activities, to developing a complex design that compares the effect on participants of different strategies or techniques. In either of these cases, you are interested in the results of the intervention on the recipients. Figure 6.1 illustrates the conceptual framework for developing a results-based evaluation plan.

FOUR STEPS OF PREPARING
THE EVALUATION PLAN

We have identified four steps of preparing a results-focused evaluation plan to will assist you in identifying the major components and activities when developing the proposal. Our discussion will intentionally be cursory; for a more in-depth discussion, consult our references. The steps are:

1. State the expected outcomes or results.
2. Determine the type of evidence needed.
3. Develop a data collection plan.
4. Identify data analysis and reporting procedures.

Step 1: State the Expected Outcomes or Results

As we discussed in Chapter 5, your understanding of the symptoms and the causes of the need/problem lead to the development of overarching goals. These goals are translated into measurable outcome objectives that indicate the changes or benefits to the participants. Your implementation

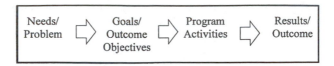

Figure 6.1. Results-Based Evaluation Framework

plan represents your theory about what will work and how it will work to achieve those changes. Well-constructed and realistic outcome objectives that are tied to reasonable time expectations are key to building a sound evaluation plan. (Refer to discussion on levels of outcomes in Chapter 5.)

Step 2: Determine the Type of Evidence Needed

The next step is to identify the evidence that represents the achievement of the outcome objectives. Often referred to as *indicators,* these are measures used to observe or quantify the outcomes. You should use indicators that are appropriate for the level of outcomes being measured—short-term or initial, intermediate, or long-term outcomes. They must be unambiguous so that one can clearly identify whether a particular instance meets the objective or not. Phrases such as "much improved" or "highly successful" may be part of your outcome objective, but they do not provide enough specificity for measurement.

Determining the appropriate measures that represent the expected results takes time and a thorough understanding of what changes your approach will yield. When working in partnership with other organizations, it is especially important that there be agreement on the best approaches for determining whether the results were achieved. Questions such as "How will we know it when we see it?" or "What are the developmental stages toward the ultimate change desired?" or "How can we tell if knowledge, attitudes, behavior, skills, or conditions have changed?" can stimulate your thinking toward developing realistic and specific indicators. In recent years, there have been compilations of indicators typically used in human services programming (see "Performance Indicators" under "Additional Suggested Readings" at the end of this book).

Table 6.1 provides examples of common indicators. In these examples, you will note that there may be more than one indicator to measure an outcome. Often, over the short term, you may increase participants' knowledge about a subject, but in the long run and more important, you will need this to result in a change in behavior or conditions.

TABLE 6.1   Common Indicators

Healthy Births
Increased knowledge about prenatal care
Lower rates of low-birth-weight babies
Higher rates of prenatal care in the first trimester

Reduced Substance Abuse
Increased knowledge about the dangers of alcohol and drug use
Percentage of youth in Grades 7-12 who consumed fewer than five or more drinks
   of alcohol on a single occasion in the last 30 days

Improved Parent Functioning
Improved scores on parenting skills pre- and posttests
Increased time spent reading to children
Employment of nonviolent techniques of disciplining

Step 3: Develop a Data Collection Plan

Once you know the specific observable measures or the type of data you will use to indicate whether an outcome has been achieved, you must develop a plan for collecting data on the indicators. Be sure to consider cultural factors when developing your data collection strategies. Such factors as cultural response sets, interpretation of the meaning of words, and mistrust or suspicion of how data will be used can affect the reliability of your results. There are several components, as shown in Figure 6.2.

When determining the data sources, consider the level of effort and cost involved. Some data may be readily accessible and in a form that you can easily use. In other cases, more effort is needed to retrieve the data. Sources for data include

- Agency records
- Progress reports
- Time allocation records
- Agendas and minutes of meetings
- Activity schedules, agency calendars
- Telephone call slips
- Visitors' logs
- Written requests for service or product
- Audio or videotapes
- Questionnaires, interview notes, program participant survey forms
- Standardized tests
- Staff notes and documentation of role plays, observations

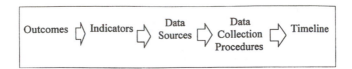

Figure 6.2. Data Collection Plan

- Service recipient intake and exit interviews
- Communitywide demographic data

The procedures for collecting the data and selecting a sample (if applicable) must also be considered. This means determining

1. Persons responsible for developing or selecting the data collection tools
2. How the data will be collected
3. Whether measurements will also be conducted on comparison/control group(s)
4. Whether the measurements are culturally competent
5. Procedures for ensuring voluntary participation in the evaluation
6. Safeguards for protecting client confidentiality
7. Sampling plans, including type of sample, and size

Another dimension to consider is the points in time that you will collect data. These data collection points should also be indicated on the project time line. When considering the timing of the measurements, think about the benefits of collecting data

- Before the project—to establish a baseline
- During the project—to monitor progress and reveal interim outcomes
- After the project—to show change and short-term outcomes through comparison with baseline data
- Follow-up, post project—to determine the long-term benefits

Step 4: Identify Data Analysis and Reporting Procedures

Review the evaluation plan to determine how you will represent the data. Do you want to show frequencies, percentages, rates, comparisons? Will you compare the outcomes of different subgroups by sociodemographic characteristics—for example, gender, age, ethnicity, income levels, and/or by the amount of exposure to the project? Which statistical techniques will be most conducive to answering the evaluation questions? Review your evaluation instruments to ensure that you have included all of the variables you may need and an appropriate method to obtain the data so that you gain maximum benefit from the effort.

Evaluation data are usually presented to the funder on either a quarterly or a semiannual basis and at the project's end. Unless the funder specifies the reporting requirements, you should decide how you will keep the funder apprised of the program's activities and accomplishments.

WRITING THE EVALUATION SECTION

The decisions made about the evaluation design must be incorporated into a coherent presentation. As with the project narrative of the proposal, funders have different expectations and requirements for writing the evaluation plan. Some will desire an elaborate narrative description, whereas others will request a brief outline or Scope of Work format. We shall discuss both formats.

NARRATIVE DESCRIPTION

If no specific instructions have been given for preparing this section, the following is a typical outline format. The decisions made during the conceptualization of the evaluation are now evidenced within this framework:

   I. Identify the evaluation goals
  II. Describe the evaluation design
 III. Identify what will be measured
  IV. Describe the data collection plan
       A. Indicators or type of data
       B. Source of data
       C. Data collection procedures
       D. Timetable
   V. Identify sampling plan (if applicable)
  VI. Discuss data analysis techniques
 VII. Address protection of human subjects and cultural relevancy
VIII. Explain staffing and management plans for the evaluation
  IX. Identify reporting procedures
   X. Show proposed budget

SCOPE OF WORK

In some instances, the funder will provide forms or require a brief outline of the evaluation plan. Completion of the Scope of Work form or some similar format may be the only requirement for describing the plans for measuring process and outcomes. This shorter representation generally entails a listing of (a) the objectives, (b) implementation activities, and (c) the types of measurements of outcome/process for each objective.

OTHER EVALUATION CONSIDERATIONS

This chapter assists you in preparing an evaluation plan for the proposal to measure process and outcome objectives. There are other considerations that may not be addressed in the proposal but should be weighed when conducting an evaluation.

In examining what was accomplished (outcome) or how it was achieved (process), one may also need to evaluate the rationale or premise on which the program was implemented. You may find that your initial understanding of the need/problem, your perceptions of the needed solutions, your organization's capacity, and/or the community's response did not yield the expected result. Your evaluation may call into question the appropriateness of the program's goals. The goals may not "fit" within the community, cultural, or organizational context. Such analysis and feedback can help to strengthen subsequent planning and implementation. This can be especially challenging when you are working as part of a collaborative, for it is difficult to untangle the individual contribution of a single organization. It is the cumulative and interactive effect of the approaches used that is being measured. Constant monitoring and shared feedback must be provided as the program unfolds.

An evaluation may exclude an assessment of the service delivery process and structure unless it is specifically stated as an objective. Yet unintended benefits and/or impediments to assessing the service delivery system may result from project strategies and activities. For example, one dimension in identifying the need/problem is to consider potential service barriers, such as availability, accessibility, awareness, acceptability, and appropriateness. Developing an evaluation plan that analyzes whether and how the project addressed these factors could reveal serendipitous benefits or unanticipated obstacles.

REMINDERS

Always be aware that the evaluation can uncover indirect benefits of the project. Such information can be useful in expanding the program and identifying the full benefits of the approach being used. It can also be useful when seeking additional funding support.

As is the case in other phases of the project, there may be constraints on the research design. In human services, many factors go into shaping the final plan, such as clients' language skills, length of time with clients, clients' willingness to participate in the evaluation, even volunteers' willingness to administer the evaluation. The environment in which the service is provided will also affect your ability to evaluate it. For example, if you hold a large public meeting and hope to pass out questionnaires, you will find that most people will carry them home with them, whereas if you are in a contained environment such as a classroom, you will have better control on the return.

Another constraint on the evaluation is that it does take a great deal of staff time in planning, administering, and evaluating the results; in other words, it costs money. Often, evaluation is kept simple to keep overall costs down. Ethical considerations can shape the evaluation plan as well. Depending on the type of research you desire, you may need to obtain client consent, to deal with issues of confidentiality or anonymity, or to obtain parental consent if asking questions of a minor. Again, it is important to keep the clients' interest foremost in your mind and respect their right to privacy as you design the evaluation. If you are concerned about possible ethical issues in your evaluation, check your library or a local university for research guidelines with human subjects before proceeding.

Most major universities have research departments. It is often possible for nonprofit agencies to connect with individuals who have specific expertise in evaluation and solicit their involvement in the project. The benefits of having a professional researcher assist with the evaluation design are obvious, and if it is at all possible, we recommend that you seek that expertise if you are not familiar with evaluation methodologies.

Keep the evaluation plan within the reach of the expertise of the staff. The easier it is to implement and analyze the evaluation, the more likely you are to be successful. It is essential that you involve the staff in developing the evaluation plan. Also, feedback from other professionals in direct contact with similar clients may reveal variables that you had not considered. Evaluation can be very rewarding for the agency and, ultimately, for those you serve!

7

CREATING THE BUDGET

Chapter Highlights

- ◆ Types of Budgets
- ◆ Budgeting for the First-Time Grantwriter
- ◆ Other Budget Issues

This chapter is divided into three sections. The first differentiates three major types of budgets. The second is written for the first-time proposal writer and proceeds on a step-by-step basis through the preparation of a line-item budget. The final section discusses budget issues, including the preparation of a simplified budget for foundation and corporate grants, budget adjustments and amendments, contract negotiations, and subcontracting considerations.

TYPES OF BUDGETS

The cost of running a program is expressed in a budget. As discussed in other chapters of this book, the program and the budget are closely tied to one another: A program costs money, and the budget tells how much it will cost and how the money is to be spent. For the most part, you need not be a financial wizard to develop a budget for a program; however, you will need to allow enough time to do the research to develop the budget wisely.

Budgeting for nonprofit organizations is becoming increasingly complex. Agencies are asked to respond to different funders' fiscal requirements and procedures, thus placing increased demands on agency accountants, bookkeepers, and administrators. The demands for accountability and justification of resources are requiring different ways of viewing and categorizing funds. It is no longer sufficient for agency administrators to indicate what monies are being spent *on*; they are also being asked to describe what moneys are being spent *for*, that is, for what purpose or result.

Budgets are further complicated by multiple funding sources for a single project or by elaborate subcontracting arrangements with collaborative or partner agencies. (For further reading, we recommend Kettner, Moroney, & Martin, 1990.)

There are different types of budgets. *Line item budgets,* which are discussed in detail later in this chapter, are most commonly required by funders. They represent the expenditures in specific budget categories (e.g., personnel and nonpersonnel). Two other budget types, *performance or functional budgets* and *program budgets,* go beyond itemizing expenditures to providing information that can assist in the efficient management and allocation of financial resources. They help to provide useful feedback about the costs of project activities and program objectives. A brief overview of functional and program budgets follows. (For more detailed explanations of budgeting and financial management for nonprofits, see Bryce, 1987; Vinter & Kish, 1984; Wacht, 1984.)

A simplified version of a line-item budget is presented in Table 7.1. A total amount is developed for each budget line item, and they are all added together to create a project total.

A functional or program budget organizes expenditures according to a specific agency program or by a project's objectives. From a properly constructed functional budget, one is able to determine the costs of performing certain units of work (Lauffer, 1997). Thus, one is able to ascertain the cost differentials between objectives. The functional budget example provided below in Table 7.2 looks at the costs associated with achieving each objective of the program.

To summarize, the functional budget in Table 7.2 represents the combined subtotals of the activities ($20,150 + $16,450 + $19,575 + $13,270). The program budget is the total budgeted cost for Objective A ($39,725) and Objective B ($29,720). Both budgets are necessarily equal to the line-item budget total in Table 7.1 of $69,445. Presenting the budgets in this manner provides an "at-a-glance" comparative analysis of the project's competing functions and objectives.

Some funders will provide an actual form on which to submit the budget request. The form provided in Table 7.3 is a copy of the federal budget form called Standard Form 424A; interestingly enough, it can be used to

TABLE 7.1 Simplified Line-Item Budget for Geta Grant Agency's Learning for Life Project, July 1, 20xx, to June 30, 20xx

Budget Category	Total Budget Request (in Dollars)
Personnel	$41,500.
Supplies and Materials	15,250.
Printing	7,395.
Facilities	3,650.
Equipment	1,650.
Project Total	**$69,445.**

TABLE 7.2 Relationship Between Functional Budget and Program Budget for the Learning for Life Project

	Program Budget		
Functional Budget Activities	Objective A: Parents	Objective B: Teens	Total
(1) Develop Training Curriculum			
Line Items			
Personnel	$10,000.	$8,000.	$18,000.
Supplies and Materials	5,000.	4,000.	9,000.
Printing	3,000.	3,000.	6,000.
Facilities	1,500.	1,000.	2,500.
Equipment	650.	450.	1,000.
Activity #1 Subtotal	$20,150.	$16,450.	$36,600.
(2) Conduct Training and Groups			
Personnel	$15,000.	$8,500.	$23,500.
Supplies/Materials	3,500.	2,750.	6,250.
Printing	450.	945.	1,395.
Facilities	350.	800.	1,150.
Equipment	275.	275.	550.
Activity #2 Subtotal	$19,575.	$13,270.	$32,845.
Total Project	**$39,725.**	**$29,720.**	**$69,445.**

provide a program budget or a functional budget. There are general instructions for the form and specific instructions in the RFP for the type of project request you are submitting. Although you may be able to determine how to fill this out, we recommend that for your first encounter with the form you consult with someone who is familiar with it (an accountant or agency personnel, perhaps).

TABLE 7.3 Federal Budget Form (Standard Form 424A)

BUDGET INFORMATION - Non-Construction Programs

OMB Approval No. 0348-0044

SECTION A - BUDGET SUMMARY

Grant Program Function or Activity (a)	Catalog of Federal Domestic Assistance Number (b)	Estimated Unobligated Funds		New or Revised Budget		
		Federal (c)	Non-Federal (d)	Federal (e)	Non-Federal (f)	Total (g)
1.		$	$	$	$	$
2.						
3.						
4.						
5. Totals		$	$	$	$	$

SECTION B - BUDGET CATEGORIES

6. Object Class Categories	GRANT PROGRAM, FUNCTION OR ACTIVITY				Total (5)
	(1)	(2)	(3)	(4)	
a. Personnel	$	$	$	$	$
b. Fringe Benefits					
c. Travel					
d. Equipment					
e. Supplies					
f. Contractual					
g. Construction					
h. Other					
i. Total Direct Charges *(sum of 6a-6h)*					
j. Indirect Charges					
k. TOTALS *(sum of 6i and 6j)*	$	$	$	$	$
7. Program Income	$	$	$	$	$

Previous Edition Usable

TABLE 7.3 Federal Budget Form (Standard Form 424A) (Continued)

SECTION C - NON-FEDERAL RESOURCES				
(a) Grant Program	(b) Applicant	(c) State	(d) Other Sources	(e) TOTALS
8.	$	$	$	$
9.				
10.				
11.				
12. TOTAL *(sum of lines 8-11)*	$	$	$	$

SECTION D - FORECASTED CASH NEEDS				
	Total for 1st Year	1st Quarter	2nd Quarter	3rd Quarter	4th Quarter
13. Federal	$	$	$	$	$
14. Non-Federal					
15. TOTAL *(sum of lines 13 and 14)*	$	$	$	$	$

SECTION E - BUDGET ESTIMATES OF FEDERAL FUNDS NEEDED FOR BALANCE OF THE PROJECT				
(a) Grant Program	FUTURE FUNDING PERIODS (Years)			
	(b) First	(c) Second	(d) Third	(e) Fourth
16.	$	$	$	$
17.				
18.				
19.				
20. TOTAL *(sum of lines 16-19)*	$	$	$	$

SECTION F - OTHER BUDGET INFORMATION	
21. Direct Charges:	22. Indirect Charges:
23. Remarks:	

71

BUDGETING FOR THE FIRST-TIME GRANTWRITER

The most common budget format for expressing expenditures in each of these categories is a line-item budget, where each expenditure is itemized under its appropriate category. In general, costs for a project are divided into two main budget categories: personnel costs and operating expenses. Personnel costs include the salaries and benefits of the staff required to do the project, as well as consultants. Operating expenses include nonpersonnel expenditures such as rent, printing, mailing, travel, telephone, utilities, and office supplies.

The project on which you are working will probably be one program or the entire agency picture. It will represent a percentage of the agency's total program. If this is the case, the agency will establish a fund (an account) to receive and spend the money for this particular project. The agency will also divide certain costs among the different funds it receives, usually according to the percentage that the fund represents of the total agency budget. A simple way to understand this is to consider the issue of paying the rent. If there are four sources of money coming into the agency of equal amounts, the agency could charge each fund 25% of the rent. If the proposal you are writing will be the only source of income to the agency, rent will be charged at 100%.

If you are working for a large agency, these accounting practices will be well established, and the accounting department can tell you exactly what it will cost the agency to run the program. Give the accountant or controller specific information regarding your program's use of the agency's resources. For example, estimate the number of copies you will make on the agency's copy machine during the project year, the number of pieces of mail you will send out, the cost of phone calls, and so on. In addition, if you are working for a large agency, you can rely on in-house expertise in determining program costs, and you will have an already established salary range for employees. Plan to allow enough time for the accountant to respond to your requests to provide actual cost figures based on your projected use of resources.

If you are writing the budget for a new agency or a very small agency, there may not be an accountant on whom you can depend. There may be no predetermined salary range for the personnel you propose to hire, and there may be no estimates of the costs of telephone or copier service. The job of writing the budget now becomes a bit more complex, and you must determine what this program will cost. The remainder of this chapter is be devoted to the grantwriter who has little or no support to develop the budget. How does one begin? The following discussions will take you step by step through determining personnel costs.

PERSONNEL COSTS

Types of Staff Needed

What kind of staff do you need to run the project? Must they be professionally trained in the field? Can student interns be used? What clerical staff are needed? Write down each type of staff person you will need.

Time Required in Each Personnel Category

Now you want to determine the amount of time that the project will require of each specific staff position. This time is often referred to in terms of *full-time equivalents* (FTEs) and is expressed as a decimal. A 1.00 FTE represents the total amount of paid service that is the equivalent of one person working full time for 12 months. Any figure less than 1.00 always states the decimal *proportion* of a 12-month full-time job for which the person or persons have been employed (Vinter & Kish, 1984, p. 367). In some cases, you may see a request for the *percentage of time,* which is expressed as a percentage. For example, if you are using percentage of time and have a need for a half-time employee, the position would be for 50% time, or .50 FTEs. (See Appendix A for a discussion on estimating staff time.)

Determining Salaries

Determining salaries can be a difficult task. You may need to do some research into the local marketplace to see what people in comparable positions are earning, and there are published reports on compensation in nonprofit agencies. (For more help, contact your local nonprofit resource center or association.) You may also get some sense of appropriate salary range in the classified ads of the local newspaper. Once you have these data, consider any special skills that may be required as well as what you think is "fair" reimbursement for the effort.

At this point, we also want to point out that the "poverty mentality" of social services is changing. In the past, social services paid notoriously little in return for the education and experience required to do the work. Most agencies have found that it is difficult to attract and keep top-quality people in the nonprofit arena. They have had to contend with a high attrition rate, which costs the agency time, service, and money over the long run. Most funders today are well aware of the need to hire excellent staff in order to run a sound program and are willing to support it.

PERSONNEL BUDGET EXAMPLE

Table 7.4 shows how each of the staff categories has been itemized, along with an indication of the FTEs, the fixed monthly full-time salary range, and the total requested amount for a 1-year period. (Note also that the FTE has an asterisk by it referring to a footnote stating that "the FTE is subject to change during the contract year." This will provide some flexibility in the contract in case there is a vacancy in the position or some other need to deviate slightly from the stated time commitment. We have found this to be a part of some state contracts but not others, so just be aware that it exists.)

As shown in Table 7.4, employee benefits are also included under "Personnel Costs." It is up to the agency to determine what is included in this benefits line. At a minimum, this amount will include employer contributions for federal and state governments (e.g., taxes, unemployment insurance, social security contributions). Employee benefits may also cover health and dental insurance and retirement funds. The amount of benefit is calculated as a percent of total salary.

OPERATING EXPENSES

Now let us look at the second section of the budget, which addresses operating expenses. Again, it is important to look carefully at the proposal itself and identify all of the items that will cost money. The budget categories listed in Table 7.5 are typical among project proposals.

Many state and federal funders have established fixed reimbursement rates for such things as mileage, per diem expenses, and consultants. Many will not allow for food costs in association with any training you may want to conduct. For the beginning grantwriter, it may be helpful to contact the executive director of a similar type of agency for assistance with this category. Another option is to contact a local grantsmanship center or a university grants department and ask for the most current reimbursement rates in your state or to contact the state board of control that fixes the rates on a yearly basis. (You might be asking, "Why don't I call the state or federal office to which I am applying for funds to get the information?" Because you will look like a beginner, and your position in the eyes of the funder

TABLE 7.4 Personnel Budget of the Learning for Life Project

Personnel	FTE[a]	Salary Range (Month)	Total
Executive Director	.05	$4,500-$5,500	$3,000.
Project Director	1.0	3,000-4,000	42,000.
Clerical	.50	2,000-2,400	12,522.
Subtotal Salaries			$57,522.
Benefits @ 20%			11,504.
Total Personnel			$69,026.

a. FTE is subject to change over the contract year.

TABLE 7.5 Operating Expenses of the Learning for Life Project

Operating Expenses	Total
Rent (600 sq. ft. @ 1.30 per sq. ft. x 12 months)	$9,360.
Printing	2,800.
Equipment Rental and Maintenance	3,200.
Telephone	2,400.
Travel	2,580.
Subtotal Operating Expenses	$22,140.

may be weakened. Try to discover the answers to the above questions on your own first, and if that fails, then call the funder.)

Other details in the budget will not be apparent until you reach the negotiation stage. For example, you might have $5,000 in the budget to purchase a computer and printer. During the negotiations, if the funder tells you that they will not pay for the purchase of equipment but will allow you to rent it, you can then make the necessary adjustments. *Read* all of the instructions the funder gives on preparing the budget. Most funders state their restrictions in their application package. Now we combine both the personnel and operating expenses and have a typical format (Table 7.6) for project budget requests to the state.

BUDGET JUSTIFICATIONS

In addition to writing the line-item budget, many funders want an even more detailed description of what is included on each line and how the totals per line were reached. In a budget justification, each of the lines is explained. The following is an example of a budget justification:

TABLE 7.6   Typical Budget Format, Learning for Life Project

	FTE[a]	Salary Range (Month)	Total
Personnel			
Executive Director	.05	$4,500-5,500	$3,000.
Project Director	1.0	3,000-4,000	42,000.
Clerical	.50	2,000-$2,400	12,522.
Subtotal Salaries			$57,522.
Benefits @ 20%			11,504.
Total Personnel			$69,026.
Operating Expenses			
Rent (600 sq. ft. @ 1.30 per sq. ft. x 12 months)			$9,360.
Office Supplies			1,800.
Printing			2,800.
Equipment Rental and Maintenance			3,200.
Telephone			2,400.
Travel			2,580.
Subtotal Operating Expenses			$22,140.
Total Budget Request			**$91,166.**

a. FTE is subject to change over the contract year.

Budget Justification for Geta Grant Agency

Personnel

Executive Director: The executive director will be responsible for the supervision of staff, a small part of community networking, and overall program management, representing .05 FTE, for a total of $3,000.

Project Director will work full time (100%) on this project, with program implementation and evaluation responsibilities, staff and volunteer supervision, and report-writing duties. The salary is $42,000 per year.

Clerical: A clerk will be assigned 50% time on this project to prepare project correspondence, make phone calls to schedule programs, and respond to questions or requests for information. The salary is $12,522 per year.

Employee benefits have been calculated at 20%, which includes FICA and federal withholding, SDI, state withholding, workers' compensation, and health and dental benefits. The benefits for this project total $14,000.

Operating Expenses

Rent has been calculated at $1.30 per square foot times 600 square feet of space, for a total of $780 per month times 12 months, or $9,360. Utilities are included.

Phone costs are calculated at $200 per month times 12 months, for a total of $24,000 per year.

Travel expenses include mileage to and from school sites and community meeting places for an estimated 555 miles per month at 26 cents per mile times 12 months, for a total of $1,730. Also included in travel is $850 for transportation and per diem (at state board of control rates) to one major conference for two staff members. The total request for travel is $2,580.

OTHER BUDGETING ISSUES

SIMPLIFIED BUDGETS

Some foundations and nonprofit trusts require a more simplified budget in which you indicate expense categories rather than itemizing line by line. The budget in Table 7.7 places line-item categories into more general categories. This type of budget provides the agency with much more flexibility in the actual allocation of expenses, and it is usually possible for the agency to transfer funds between lines without contacting the funder.

MATCHING FUNDS AND IN-KIND BUDGETS

When some of the costs of the project will be assumed by the agency, the agency is said to be contributing this money "in kind," and this portion of agency-borne expense is indicated in the budget. Some funding sources may require that the agency provide matching funds of a certain percentage of the amount requested. For example, one state office offered to fund 75% of the cost of providing a case management system to pregnant and parenting teens. The applicant had to provide a 25% match.

One program director we interviewed called "in-kind" contributions "the creative writing section of the proposal." Examples of in-kind contributions are volunteer time dedicated to this project, donated goods or services, and funds leveraged from another source that are devoted to these services. The funds need to be focused on the services of this grant and, for the most part, cannot count as matching funds if they are paying for other services or if the clients who are receiving the services will be reported to another funder. (This is called "double counting" and is prohibited in most situations.)

Table 7.8 indicates one way to present an in-kind budget. The first column indicates the funder's portion of the total request, the second column indicates the agency's portion, and the third column indicates the total to be allocated for each item. Note: A similar format can be used if you are writing a proposal in which the resources are coming from more than one

TABLE 7.7   Foundation or Corporate Budget, Learning for Life Project

Personnel	
Salaries	$57,522.
Benefits @ 20%	11,504.
Total Personnel	$69,026.
Operating Expenses	
Overhead Costs (Rent, Phone, Utilities)	$14,960.
Program Expenses (Supplies, Videos, Printing)	4,600.
Travel and Conferences	2,580.
Subtotal Operating Expenses	$22,140.
Total Budget Request	**$91,166.**

TABLE 7.8   In-Kind Budget, Learning for Life Project

	FTE[a]	Salary Range (Month)	Funding Request	Agency In-Kind	Total
Personnel					
Executive Director	.05	$4,500-$5,500	$2,000.	$1,000	$3,000.
Project Director	1.0	3,000-4,000	38,000.	4,000.	42,000.
Clerical	.50	2,000-$2,400	12,522.	0	12,522.
Accounting	.10	3,100-4,200	0	4,800.	4,800.
Subtotal Salaries			$52,522.	9,800.	$62,322.
Benefits @ 20%			10,504.	1,960.	12,464.
Total Personnel			$63,026.	$11,760.	$74,786.
Operating Expenses					
Rent			4,000.	5,360.	$9,360.
Office Supplies			1,500.	300.	1,800.
Printing			2,200.	600.	2,800.
Equipment Rental and Maintenance			2,800.	400.	3,200.
Telephone			2,000.	400.	2,400.
Travel			2,000.	580.	2,580.
Subtotal Operating Expenses			$14,500.	$7,640.	$22,140.
Total Budget Request			**$77,526.**	**$19,400.**	**$976,926.**

funder. Indicate the source of the funding in each column, followed by a total funding column.

BUDGET ADJUSTMENTS

In the line-item budget, the agency is accounting for expenses on a per-line basis. Most funders with line-item budgets do not allow the agency to

TABLE 7.9 Budget Adjustment

	Prior Approved Amount	Adjustment Effective 10/1/20xx	New Approved Amount
Personnel			
Executive Director	$2,000.	(100)	$1,900.
Project Director	38,000.	0	38,000.
Clerical	12,522.	0	12,522.
Benefits	10,504.	(20)	10,484.
Total Personnel	$52,522.	(120)	$52,502.
Operating Expenses			
Rent	$4,000.	0	$4,000.
Office Supplies	1,500.	500.	2,000.
Printing	2,200.	(380)	1,820.
Equipment Rental and Maintenance	2,800.	(500)	2,300.
Telephone	2,000.	0	2,000.
Travel	2,000.	500.	2,500.
Subtotal Operating Expenses	14,500.	120.	14,500.
Total Budget	**$77,526.**	**0**	**$77,526.**

transfer funds between lines without their consent. This process of requesting a transfer between lines is called a *budget adjustment.*

Table 7.9 is an example of how a budget adjustment is presented. One column lists the current contract totals for the year, another indicates the amount of money you want to add or subtract from the column, and the final column indicates the new totals. With budget adjustments, you are not changing the total amount that you have to work with, just reallocating the money between lines.

The adjusted budget will most often need to have a written explanation attached that describes what has happened, on a per-line basis, to necessitate the request for a change. In the explanation, you will tell the funder why there is excess money in some lines and why there is a deficit in others. The funder will be looking for a legitimate rationale to move funds between lines.

BUDGET AMENDMENTS

If, during the course of the contract, your scope of work has been expanded or reduced, you may need to do a budget amendment reflecting this change. A simple way to think about this is: When you need to shift money and it does not alter the scope of work in any way, you write an adjustment. If something has happened to significantly alter the scope —for example, the funder has asked you to take on an additional project or activity and will provide more money—you write an amendment. Some funders require an amendment if you are seeking to move more than $5,000 (or some other predetermined amount). Amendments are usually written using the same budget format for requesting adjustments.

The major difference between an amendment and an adjustment is that the amendment changes your contract with the funder and goes through a formal approval process. You will receive a new copy of the contract with the amended budget and any program changes resulting from the amendment.

CONTRACT NEGOTIATIONS

When you negotiate a contract with a funder, be most conscious of the possible "domino" effect that one change in program will have on the entire program and the impact it will have on the budget. Most of the time, projects are designed so that the parts are interrelated and interconnected. Changing what appears to be one aspect of the project can have considerable effect on the whole.

Upon approving the proposal, some funders conduct formal contract negotiations. The negotiation is a time when you meet face to face, review what is going to be provided by the contract, and discuss a rationale for the implementation activities, the objectives, or perhaps even the goals. The funder may want to change an objective, increase the numbers, add a new objective, or clarify certain language. Most often, the funder approves the proposal for a lesser amount of money than you requested: For example, your request may have been for $175,000, but the funder allocates only $160,000.

A little caveat to first-time grantwriters: You will be very excited that you have been funded. So excited, in fact, that you may be willing to do anything just to get the money and get the project started. *Be careful.* You can damage your project in the negotiations. The funder has a commitment to fund the project and will want the most for its money. No one knows the project better than you. Approach the negotiations from the perspective of Win-Win. The funder wants a good program just as you do. Here are a few guidelines for negotiating contracts:

1. Reread the proposal just prior to going into the negotiations. Be as intimately familiar with all of it as you were when you were writing it 6 months ago.

2. Create an atmosphere of partnership with the contract negotiator.
3. Take your time when you make changes. Look at the impact any change will have on the objectives.
4. Be prepared to discuss your rationale for keeping the project as initially developed in the proposal.
5. If the agency has not been awarded the full amount requested, prepare a new version of the proposal in advance of the meeting. This gives you time to rethink the budget and program and decide on revisions.
6. Remember to maintain your integrity. If you know that the agency cannot do the job for the amount of money offered, despite changes to make it more cost-effective, the agency will need to decide if it is worth pursuing. It is possible, and we have seen it happen, that the agency will choose to turn down the contract because accepting it would be too costly to the agency.

SUBCONTRACTING

Subcontracting means contracting with another agency to provide a portion of the service in the proposal. Your agency receives the contract, and under that contract, you also have a contractual arrangement with another agency to deliver a service. This is a typical arrangement used by collaboratives. The subcontracting agency is bound by the same contractual terms as the primary contractor. The primary contractor is responsible for ensuring that the subcontracting agency abides by the terms of the contract and usually prepares a legally binding agreement with the subcontractor. (For a more in-depth treatment of the topic of contracts and subcontracting, see Kettner & Martin, 1987.)

If you are using subcontractors, you have to address this issue within the body of the grant itself to clearly identify by objectives the role of the subcontractor in the contract and to establish the credibility of the subcontractor in the applicant capability section. The budget of the subcontractor is included in the main budget and fully described in the budget justification.

As you review the steps in budget preparation, you can see why it should not be left to the last minute. Preparing the budget requires that you have a thorough grasp of the project, including all of the details of the implementation activities, so that you can be certain not to omit any major costs. Remember: Changes in the program will have an impact on the budget, and changes in the budget will have an impact on the program.

AGENCY CAPABILITY
AND FINISHING TOUCHES

Chapter Highlights

- ◆ The Agency Capability Statement
- ◆ Requesting Letters of Support
- ◆ The Proposal Abstract
- ◆ The Title and Title Page
- ◆ The Cover Letter

THE AGENCY CAPABILITY STATEMENT

The agency capability statement establishes an organization's credibility to successfully undertake the project. It indicates who is applying for the grant, what qualifies an agency to conduct the project, and what resources (e.g., organizational, community) are available to support the effort. This section helps to generate confidence that the agency is programmatically competent and qualified to address the needs/problem and is fiscally sound and responsible.

In developing this section, the grantwriter must reflect the agency's image of itself as well as the constituency's image of it. This includes describing the organization's unique contributions to those it serves and capturing the community's regard for these contributions. When preparing this section, one should provide quantitative evidence of the agency's accomplishments. A recurring weakness in capability statements is observed when the agency makes qualitative assessments of the organization without some corroborating data to support the claims.

A capability statement should accomplish two things: (a) It should describe the agency's characteristics and its track record, and (b) it should demonstrate how those qualities make the agency qualified to undertake the proposed project. Many times, grantwriters accomplish the first task but leave it up to the reviewers to infer the latter. They often fail to present a cogent argument that connects what they have done with what they are now proposing to do (see Chapter 2).

When writing this section, avoid overusing the words *we* and *our.* It is appropriate to refer to the name of the agency or simply say "the agency" throughout the text. Write as if you are developing a public relations article for a national newsletter, informing the reader, making it interesting but brief. A typical agency capability statement will reflect much of the following information:

1. *Mission of the Agency*—the overall philosophy and aims of the organization
2. *History of the Agency*—a brief overview of when, why, and how the agency started and whether its focus has changed over time.
3. *Organizational Resources*—a description of the agency's funding track record and of the human and material resources available to this project. (Include the pertinent background of staff, especially expertise in areas related to the needs/problem, other professionals associated with the agency, and any special equipment, materials, and services that can support the proposed project.)
4. *Community Recognition and Support*—an indication of how the agency is regarded, including awards, accreditations, and honors bestowed upon it and the staff, as well as how the community is involved in the agency's operation and structure (e.g., through membership, in programs, on committees and boards).
5. *Interagency Collaboration and Linkages*—a depiction of the linkages and support available from other organizations that can assist with the proposed project, including memberships in local, state, and national networks.
6. *Agency Programs*—an overview of the unique programmatic contributions the agency makes to its clients and the community, including the aims and types of programs, and a quantitative picture of what is accomplished (e.g., the numbers served, the distribution rate of materials, the cost savings resulting from these services).
7. *Agency Strengths*—a description of the organizational characteristics that make the agency particularly suited to implement the project. In general, you indicate what is being proposed and how that fits with what the organization already has accomplished. For example, the agency may already be serving the target group, addressing the needs/problem, or using a particular technique or strategy that it now wishes to modify or implement differently.

SUPPORTIVE DOCUMENTATION

Depending on the funder, you may be expected to provide documentation on the agency's capability. These materials are usually placed in an appendix to the application. Be selective in the type of documentation you incorporate into the proposal. Typical examples include

- Letters of cooperation from other organizations
- Letters from other agencies or professionals attesting to the merits of the agency and the proposed project
- Letters from the agency's constituency (such as clients indicating the importance of this project to themselves and others in similar situations)
- Copies of documents demonstrating agency accomplishments, including awards and recognition from local, state, and national groups
- A listing of the members of the agency's board of directors and their qualifications and affiliations
- An organizational chart

REQUESTING LETTERS OF SUPPORT

Most agencies fax a letter specifically requesting support for a particular project to other agencies. Typically, in this letter you provide a brief synopsis of the proposed program, the funding source you are applying to, and specific instructions for writing the letter, including to whom the letter should be addressed and whether to mail it to your agency or the funder. Below is a sample of a request for a letter of support to other organizations:

We Need Your Support

The Geta Grant agency is applying for funding to the Office of Health and Human Services. In this proposal, we seek support for a case management system for the Families First Collaborative. Agencies included in this proposal include the Department of Education, A Fine Health Center, the Human Interaction Commission, and the Food Bank Distribution Center.

This project, called "Management for Health," provides a full-time caseworker to address the needs of the highest-risk Latino and white families in the cities of Lemon, Tangerine, and Banana. We expect that over 100 families with multiple needs will be served in the first year. In addition, our project will evaluate the effectiveness of case management with this population.

If you see the need for these services in our community, please write a letter of support addressed to: Mary Smith, Program Officer, Office of Health and Human Services, Department 007, 200 State Lane, Room 123, Our

Town, CA 90009 *but send the letter to me*: Grantwriter, Geta Grant Agency, 1111 One Street, This Town, CA 90002. We thank you for your support. Please call us to pick up the letter by Friday, June 2, 20xx.

As the grantwriter, be prepared to make follow-up phone calls to the agencies and to pick up the letter if you are nearing the proposal deadline. In some instances, you may be asked by the organizations to draft a letter of support for them. This is often ideal, as you can be very specific about the items you want emphasized by each supporting source.

THE PROPOSAL ABSTRACT

The abstract is usually written after the other sections because it gives an overview of the entire project. Unless the funder provides other instructions or forms, the abstract is typically no longer than one page. The abstract is used by the funder to screen the proposal for appropriateness in light of their funding objectives. A glance at the abstract also assists staff in disseminating the document to the proper review committees or funding offices. Once a proposal is funded, the abstract is often used by funders to convey to the public their funding decisions and activities.

Although the abstract is sometimes hurriedly written at the end, care and attention should be given to its content. This is *not* the proposal introduction; rather, it is a summary of the entire project. As such, the abstract should parallel the major sections of the proposal. An abstract will typically

1. Identify the agency requesting the funds
2. Describe the target population
3. Summarize the needs/problem statement, highlighting data that show the magnitude or extent of the problem
4. Provide a synopsis of the project objectives, including goals and objectives
5. Highlight the evaluation plan and the expected outcomes or results of the project
6. Provide an "amount requested" figure

THE TITLE AND TITLE PAGE

Develop a title that reflects the major goal(s) of the project. Although one may develop a "catchy" title, its meaning should be readily understood by the reviewers. A descriptive subtitle may be used to clarify. Avoid long titles or ones that are used too often by other projects.

A title page usually accompanies the proposal. Federal and state agencies will often provide the face sheets necessary. Although there is no standard format for the title page, the following is typical:

- Project title
- Name of the agency submitting grant
- Agency address
- Name of prospective funder
- Project begin and end dates
- Amount requested

THE COVER LETTER

A letter of transmittal on agency stationery, signed by the appropriate organizational official, should be prepared. The letter conveys interest in the funder's mandate and mission and states how the project fits within these mandates. The letter should be brief (usually one page), and it should indicate the agency's board approval of the proposal, the contact person (with telephone number), and the willingness to respond to any questions about the project. Also include a paragraph that summarizes the project.

Remember that the letter is often the first contact between the agency requesting funds and the prospective funder. Set a tone of professionalism and competency. The letter should be written on agency letterhead.

Appendix A

ESTIMATING TIME

In this section, we have provided for the beginning grantwriter an illustration of the process involved in calculating a staff person's time expenditure on a project. Let's suppose that Geta Clinic wants to provide an AIDS prevention education program in the county schools. The objective states:

Three thousand (3,000) at-risk youth will increase their knowledge by 30% on HIV transmission and risk-reduction behaviors by June 30, 20xx.

The implementation activities, with staff responsibilities include

1. Establishing a relationship with the schools (Project Director, Community Educator)
2. Developing and scheduling education programs (Community Educator, Administrative Assistant)
3. Planning and conducting Parent Orientation Nights (Community Educator)
4. Providing two 1-hour educational presentations in the students' regular classroom on the nature of HIV transmission, risky behaviors, decision-making skills, and assertiveness training (Community Educator)
5. Doing student evaluations using a pre-post test to indicate knowledge change (Community Educator and Administrative Assistant)

Someone without any knowledge about community education might say:

Okay, this is simple. An average class size would be 25. Divide 3,000 by 25 to find out how many actual classes you need; that equals 120 classes. Since the educator will spend 2 hours in each class, that is a total of 240 teaching hours. If I divide 240 hours by 8 hours per day, then I need a community educator for 30 days.

The above reasoning process is faulty for a number of reasons. What factors need to be considered when implementing a community education program for Geta Clinic? The following discussion will provide an example of the kind of "thinking-through" process needed to develop a more realistic estimate of the time it will take:

- *Access to the Community.* Has the clinic ever provided educational programs in the schools? How much time will it take to develop the necessary relationships with the schools to gain access? How much time will be spent scheduling programs? How much time in community relations to develop the network? Will the sensitive nature of the topic affect this development time by making it even more difficult to gain access to the classroom?

- *Service Preparation, Evaluation, and Documentation.* How much preparation will be required to provide the educational program in addition to the direct teaching time? Will the educator need to write the curriculum? Will he or she also need to evaluate the program's effectiveness? Grade the evaluation exams? Maintain other program records? Develop handouts for classroom use?

- *Geographic Location.* How many sites can be reached in a day? Consider the traffic patterns, distance, and climate.

- *Ethnic, Cultural, and Linguistic Considerations.* Will the clinic need educators from different ethnic backgrounds? What languages will need to be spoken? Written? Is a special knowledge required to work with the specific population(s), and if so, how much time will it take for the educator to acquire that?

- *Human Capability.* Finally, consider what is humanly possible to require of a community educator in terms of actual teaching within a given day or week. The energy required in the classroom when the speaker is an "outsider" is considerably greater than when the audience is familiar with the person. Once the program has gained access to the schools, perhaps one 2-hour presentation per day is all you can reasonably expect someone to do and maintain enthusiasm in the process.

Now it is time to recalculate the amount of time required from the educational staff. A full-time employee works 156 hours per month. You have determined that the educator will need to spend time developing relationships with the schools. You might estimate that it will take approximately 8 hours of contact time on the phone and in person per school that you want to reach. There are 50 high schools, so contacting each high school would entail about *400 hours.*

Then you calculate that it will take the educator approximately 2 to 3 weeks full time to review the available materials and to plan the curriculum. If portions of the curriculum need to be written and/or evaluation tools developed, it will take, you estimate, about 1 month. If you add that time together, it is approximately *300 hours.*

We already know that the teacher will spend 240 hours in the classroom. He or she will go to 120 different classes. If you estimate 30 minutes' travel time each way, that will be another 120 hours in traveling time. So the time spent in classroom presentations and travel time totals *360 hours.*

You have also calculated that it will take the educator approximately 1 hour per class to handle the evaluation component, which equates to another *120 hours.*

You want the educator to have a minimum of 10 hours per month to improve his or her skills and knowledge, update records, attend an in-service, and respond to correspondence; that adds up to another *120 hours.*

Finally, let's add the fact that due to the sensitive nature of the materials to be addressed in the classroom, the community educator will also need to be involved in making a presentation at Parents' Night so that they may review materials and ask questions. This will require 2 hours at 50 schools for another *100 hours* plus the hour of travel time for *50 hours.* Networking with other community groups and involvement on task forces or committees will take another 5 hours per month or *60 hours* per year.

The total number of hours involved in the community educator's work comes to *1,510 hours for the project year.* There are 1,872 hours in a work year. Some planners will tell you that once you have made your best time estimate, it is wise to take an additional 25%. The reasoning behind this is that it will always take more time than you think and there will inevitably be delays. In the case of the Geta Clinic, it appears that it would be wise to hire a full-time educator (100%) to reach 3,000 teens with an AIDS prevention program.

In the way that we have conceptualized the job now, the educator will spend the first 4 to 5 months preparing to teach and making contacts with the schools and the remaining 7 months of the project year providing the actual service. The factors we have included in calculating the amount of time an educator would spend to reach 3,000 teens should follow the implementation activities fairly closely. These calculations will also be needed as you determine the cost of the project. Often, as the true extent of time and effort needed is revealed, the implementation activities or the objectives may be modified to conform to budget restrictions.

Appendix B

FUNDING RESOURCE INFORMATION

Listed below are common sources of information on funding resources that you might find helpful. This is a selective listing; for a more complete picture of funding opportunities, you can consult your local library or contact one of the following organizations/Web sites.

ORGANIZATIONS AND WEB SITES

- *Grants, Etc.* The University of Michigan's Web site, offering access to founding sources, in-kind resources, electronic journals, how-to guides, and other valuable resources. *http://www.ssw.umich.edu/gransetc*
- *The Grantsmanship Center.* 1125 W. Sixth Street, Fifth Floor, P.O. Box 17220, Los Angeles, CA 90017. *http://www.tgci.com.* An organization that has an extensive inventory of funding information, publishes a newspaper for grant-seeking organizations, and conducts national training on proposal writing and other areas of human service administration.
- *The Foundation Center.* 79 Fifth Avenue, New York, NY 10003. *http://www.fdncenter.org.* An independent national service organization established by foundations to provide an authoritative source of information on private philanthropic giving; publishes various directories and guides on foundations; has established a national network of reference collections through local and university libraries, community foundations, and nonprofit organizations.

INTERNET ADDRESSES OF FEDERAL AND STATE FUNDERS

- Catalog of Federal Domestic Assistance: *http://www.gsa.gov/fcac*
- Federal Information Exchange: *http://www.fie.com*
- State Government Links: *http://www.law.indiana.edu/law/v-lib/states.html*

- National Institutes for Health (NIH): *http://www.nih.gov*
- U.S. Department of Health and Human Services: *http://www.dhhs.gov*
- U.S. Department of Education: *http://www.ed.gov*

MAJOR PUBLICATIONS

- *Annual Register of Grant Support.* Marquis Who's Who, 4300 West 62nd Street, Indianapolis, IN 46206.
- *Catalog of Federal Domestic Assistance.* Superintendent of Documents, Government Printing Office, Washington, DC 20402.
- *Federal Grants and Contracts Weekly.* Capitol Publications, 1300 North 17th Street, Arlington, VA 22209.
- *Federal Register.* Superintendent of Documents, Government Printing Office, Washington, DC 20402.
- *Foundation Directory, Foundation Directory Supplements, Foundation Grants Index, National Data Book of Foundations, National Guide to Funding for Children, Youth and Families, Corporate Foundation Profiles*: publications of the Foundation Center, 79 Fifth Avenue, New York, NY 10003.
- *Fund Raiser's Guide to Human Service Funding* (2nd ed.). Taft Group, 5130 MacArthur Blvd. NW, Washington, DC 20016-3316.
- *Grantsmanship Book.* Reprints from the Grantsmanship Center, 1125 W. Sixth Street, Fifth Floor, P.O. Box 17220, Los Angeles, CA 90017.

COMPUTERIZED SEARCHES
AND DATABASES

A number of computerized search services are available that provide funding resource information. The advantage of such databases is that they can subdivide and index the funding information into a range of subjects and categories (e.g., by subject, by geographic area). The costs can vary, and some of the information overlaps in the different databases. Check your local university library for more information about search services. (Library tip: If you are no longer a student and want to use a university library, check to see if they have a "Friends of the Library" program. You may be able to join the library for a reasonable amount per year through this fund-raising arm of the library.)

DIALOG Information Retrieval Service is among the largest databases covering a broad range of topics. Among the funding-related databases in the service are the following:

- Federal Index
- Federal Register Abstracts
- Federal Research in Progress
- Foundation Directory

- Foundation Grants Index
- Guide to National Foundations

Computerized searches are also useful for readily identifying literature and data for the needs/problem statement section of the proposal. One might find journal articles or other educational resources at the following search sites:

- PsychLit database
- ERIC
- Social Science Abstracts
- Medline
- Lexis-Nexis

ON-LINE JOURNALS AND NEWSLETTERS

- Chronicle of Philanthropy: *http://www.philanthropy.com*
- Foundation News and Commentary: *http://www.Cof.org/fnc/fncindex.html*
- Grantsmanship Center Magazine: *http://www.tgci.com/publications/pub.htm*

REFERENCES

Bandura, A. (1986). *Social foundations of thought and action: A social cognitive theory.* Englewood Cliffs, NJ: Prentice Hall.

Bryce, H. J. (1987). *Financial and strategic management for nonprofit organizations.* Englewood Cliffs, NJ: Prentice Hall.

Gardner, S. (1999). *Beyond collaboration to results: Hard choices in the future of services to children and families.* Fullerton, CA: Center for Collaboration for Children.

Kettner, P. M., & Martin, L. L. (1987). *Purchase of service contracting.* Newbury Park, CA: Sage.

Kettner, P. M., Moroney, R. K., & Martin, L. L. (1990). *Designing and managing programs.* Newbury Park, CA: Sage.

Kiritz, N. J. (1980). *Program planning and proposal writing.* Los Angeles: Grantsmanship Center.

Lauffer, A. (1997). *Grants, etc.: Grant getting, contracting, and fund-raising for non-profits.* (2nd ed.). Thousand Oaks, CA: Sage.

Prochaska, J. O., Norcross, J. C., & DiClemente, C. C. (1994). *Changing for good.* New York: William Morrow.

Schaefer, M. (1985). *Designing and implementing procedures for health and human services.* Beverly Hills, CA: Sage.

Schaefer, M. (1987). *Implementing change in service programs.* Newbury Park, CA: Sage.

Soriano, F. I. (1995). *Conducting needs assessments: A multidisciplinary approach.* Newbury Park, CA: Sage.

United Way of America. (1996). *Measuring program outcomes: A practical approach* (4th ed.). Available from United Way, 701 N. Fairfax Street, Alexandria, VA 22314.

Vinter, R. D., & Kish, R. K. (1984). *Budgeting for not-for-profit organizations.* New York: Free Press.

Wacht, R. F. (1984). *Financial management in non-profit organizations.* Atlanta: Georgia State University Press.

ADDITIONAL SUGGESTED READINGS

Berk, R. A., & Rossi, P. H. (1990). *Thinking about program evaluation.* Newbury Park, CA: Sage.

Center for the Study of Social Policy. (1995). *Finding the data: A start-up list of outcome measures with annotations.* Washington, DC: Improved Outcomes for Children Project.

Connell, J., Kubisch, A., Schorr, L., & Weiss, C. (1995). *New approaches to evaluating community initiatives.* Washington, DC: Aspen Institute.

Diamond, H. (1998, Fall). *A perfect union: Public-private partnerships can provide valuable services.* National Parks Forum, *40*, 4.

Dluhy, M., & Kravitz, S. (1990). *Building coalitions in the human services.* Newbury Park, CA: Sage.

Grace, K. S. (1997). *Beyond fundraising: New strategies for non-profit innovation and investment.* New York: John Wiley.

Harvard Family Research Project. (1996). *The evaluation exchange: Emerging strategies in evaluating child and family services.* Cambridge, MA: Author.

Joyaux, S. P. (1997). *Strategic fund development: Building profitable relationships that last.* Gaithersburg, MD: Aspen.

Kettner, P. M., & Martin, L. L. (1996). *Measuring the performance of human service programs.* Newbury Park, CA: Sage.

Kniffel, A. (1995, November). *Corporate sponsorship; the new direction in fundraising. American Libraries, 26,* 10.

Krueger, R. A. (1994). *Focus groups: A practical guide for applied research* (2nd ed.). Newbury Park, CA: Sage.

Melaville, A. (1997) *A guide to selecting results and indicators: Implementing results-based budgeting.* Washington, DC: Finance Project.

National Institute for Dispute Resolution. (1997, January). What cultural groups face when being evaluated. *Forum,* No. 32.

Netting, F. E., & Williams, F. G. (1997). Is there an afterlife? How to move towards self sufficiency when foundation dollars end. *Nonprofit Management and Leadership, 7,* 3.

Pietrzak, J., Rabler, M., Renner, T., Ford, L., & Gilbert, N. (1990). *Practical program evaluation.* Newbury Park, CA: Sage.

Roth, J., Brooks-Gunn, J., Murray, L., & Foster, W. (1998). *Promoting healthy adolescents: Synthesis of youth development program evaluations.* New York: Lawrence Erlbaum.

Schorr, L. (1995). *The case for shifting to results-based accountability.* Washington, DC: Center for the Study of Social Policy.

Schram, B. (1997). *Creating small scale social programs.* Thousand Oaks, CA: Sage.

Young, N., Gardner, S., & Coley, S. (1994). Getting to outcomes in integrated service delivery models. In National Center for Service Integration (Ed.), *Making a difference: Moving to outcome-based accountability for comprehensive service reforms.* Falls Church, VA: National Center for Service Integration.

Performance Indicators

Accreditation Council on Services for People With Disabilities. (1993). *Outcome based performance measures: A procedures manual.* Towson, MD: Author.

Annie E. Casey Foundation. (1995). *Kids Count data book: State profiles of child well-being.* Baltimore: Author.

Conoly, J., & Impara, J. (1995). *Mental measurements yearbook* (12th ed.). Lincoln, NE: Buros Institute of Mental Measurements.

Department of Health and Human Services. (1995-1996). *Performance measurement in selected public health programs.* Washington, DC: Public Health Service.

Kumfer, K., Shur, G., Ross, J., Bunnell, K., Librett, J., & Millward, A. (1993). *Measurement in prevention: A manual on selecting and using instruments to evaluate prevention programs.* Washington, DC: U.S. Department of Health and Human Services, Center for Substance Abuse Prevention.

Magura, S., & Moses, B. (1986). *Outcome measures for child welfare services.* Washington, DC: Child Welfare League of America.

Touliatos, J., Perlmutter, B., & Straus, M. (1990). *Handbook of family measurement techniques.* Newbury Park, CA: Sage.

U.S. Department of Health and Human Services. (1994). *Assessing drug abuse among adolescents and adults: Standardized instruments* (Clinical Report Series). Rockville, MD: Public Health Service, National Institute on Drug Abuse.

Weiss, H., & Jacobs, F. (1988). *Evaluating family programs.* New York: Aldine de Gruyter.

ABOUT THE AUTHORS

SORAYA M. COLEY is Dean of the College of Human Development and Community Service and a Professor of Human Services at California State University, Fullerton. She was in the inaugural class of 10 individuals selected as Annie E. Casey Foundation Fellows. She also completed a postdoctoral fellowship at the University of Michigan Institute for Survey Research's Program for Black Americans. She has published and made presentations on front-line workers' experiences in human services reform, results-based service delivery, and domestic violence. She provides training and consults with local and state agencies on program planning and staff development in an outcomes-focused environment. She frequently serves on proposal review panels and has taught program design, proposal writing, and program evaluation for over 15 years.

CYNTHIA A. SCHEINBERG is past Executive Director of the Coalition for Children, Adolescents, and Parents (CCAP) in Orange, California, and served as President of the Families First Collaborative from 1991 to 1999. Over the past 16 years, she has successfully written federal, state, and local-level proposals for the agency, and has extensive experience working with and leading collaboratives serving children and families. She has a doctorate in clinical psychology from Pacifica Graduate Institute in Santa Barbara, California, and a master's degree in cultural anthropology from California State University, Fullerton. She serves on the part-time faculty of the Human Services Department, where she teaches courses in program design and proposal writing, intracultural socialization, and case management. She is a Psychological Assistant in the practice of William B. Young, PhD, in Orange, California, and is the creator of a Web site for therapists at *www.therapistthings.com*.